MULTIPLE
INTELLIGENCES
IN THE CLASSROOM

WITHDRAWN

THOMAS ARMSTRONG

ASCD

Association for Supervision and Curriculum Development
Alexandria, Virginia

Copyright © 1994 by the Association for Supervision and Curriculum Development, 1250 N. Pitt St., Alexandria, VA 22314. Tel.: (703) 549-9110   FAX: (703) 549-3891.

ASCD publications present a variety of viewpoints. The views expressed or implied in this publication should not be interpreted as official positions of the Association.

Printed in the United States of America.
Cover and interior design by Karen Monaco.

Ronald S. Brandt, *Executive Editor*
Nancy Modrak, *Managing Editor, Books and Editorial Services*
Julie Houtz, *Senior Associate Editor*
Gary Bloom, *Manager, Design and Production Services*
Stephanie Justen, *Production Coordinator*
Karen Monaco, *Senior Graphic Designer*

ASCD Stock No.: 1-94055
Price: $14.95
ISBN: 0-87120-230-1

Library of Congress Cataloging-in-Publication Data

Armstrong, Thomas.
   Multiple intelligences in the classroom / Thomas Armstrong.
      p.   cm.
   Includes bibliographical references and index.
   ISBN 0-87120-230-1 : $14.95
   1. Teaching.   2. Cognitive styles.   3. Learning.   4. Intellect.
I. Association for Supervision and Curriculum Development.
II. Title.
LB1025.3.A76   1994
370.15'23—dc20   94-14325
                                                                    CIP

Multiple Intelligences in the Classroom

WITHDRAWN

The Author

Thomas Armstrong, Ph.D., is the author of several books, including *In Their Own Way, Awakening Your Child's Natural Genius,* and *7 Kinds of Smart.* He is director of Armstrong Creative Training, P.O. Box 548, Cloverdale, CA 95425. Telephone: (707) 894-4646.

Foreword

MANY EDUCATORS ARE ACQUAINTED WITH Howard Gardner's theory of multiple intelligences. They can name most if not all of his seven intelligences, and they can even give examples of how they've used them in their life. I suspect relatively few, however, have made the seven intelligences a regular part of their classroom teaching. That may change once educators begin reading *Multiple Intelligences in the Classroom,* for Thomas Armstrong does a remarkable job of translating theory into practical, accessible ideas for the classroom teacher.

With a sure hand, Armstrong guides us through Gardner's powerful theory, providing concrete examples of how it can be applied to curriculum development, teaching strategies, classroom management, assessment, special education, and other areas. Armstrong's background in special education serves him admirably; he brings an understanding to this subject that could only have come from a talented classroom teacher.

I invite you to look at multiple intelligences through the eyes of Thomas Armstrong. Once you've begun, I think you'll be inspired to give your students the opportunity to discover and explore to the fullest their many intelligences. Let the journey begin.

ARTHUR W. STELLER
ASCD President, 1994–1995

Preface

IN ADDITION TO MY OWN WRITINGS, there are now a number of guides to the theory of multiple intelligences, written by my own associates at Harvard Project Zero and by colleagues in other parts of the country. Coming from a background in special education, Thomas Armstrong was one of the first educators to write about the theory. He has always stood out in my mind because of the accuracy of his accounts, the clarity of his prose, the broad range of his references, and the teacher-friendliness of his tone.

Now he has prepared the book that you hold in your hands for members of the Association for Supervision and Curriculum Development. Displaying the Armstrong virtues that I have come to expect, this volume is a reliable and readable account of my work, directed particularly to teachers, administrators, and other educators. Armstrong has also added some nice touches of his own: the notion of a "paralyzing experience," to complement Joseph Walters' and my concept of a "crystallizing experience"; the suggestion to attend to the way that youngsters misbehave as a clue to their intelligences; some informal suggestions about how to involve youngsters in an examination of their own intelligences and how to manage one's classroom in an MI way. He has included several rough-and-ready tools that can allow one to assess one's own intellectual profile, to get a handle on the strengths and proclivities of youngsters under one's charge, and to involve youngsters in games built around MI ideas. He conveys a vivid idea of what MI classes, teaching moves, curricula, and assessments can be like. Each chapter concludes with a set of exercises to help one build on the ideas and practices that one has just read about.

As Armstrong points out in his introduction, I do not believe that there is a single royal road to an implementation of MI ideas in the classroom. I have been encouraged and edified by the wide variety of ways in which educators around the country have made use of my ideas, and I have no problem in saying "Let 100 MI schools bloom." From my perspective, the essence of the theory is to respect the many differences among people, the multiple variations in the ways that they learn, the several modes by which they can be assessed, and the almost infinite number of ways in which they can leave a mark on the world. Because Thomas Armstrong shares this vision, I am pleased that he has had the opportunity to present these ideas to you; and I hope that you in turn will be stimulated to extend them in ways that bear your own particular stamp.

—Howard Gardner

Introduction

THIS BOOK EMERGED FROM MY WORK over the past eight years in applying Howard Gardner's theory of multiple intelligences to the nuts-and-bolts issues of classroom teaching (Armstrong 1987b, 1988, 1993). I was initially attracted to the model in 1985 when I saw that it provided a language for talking about the inner gifts of children, especially those students who have accumulated labels such as "LD" and "ADD" during their school careers (Armstrong 1987a). It was as a learning disabilities specialist during the late 1970s and early 1980s that I began to feel the need to depart from what I considered a deficit-oriented paradigm in special education. I wanted to forge a new model based on what I plainly saw were the many gifts of these "disabled" children.

I didn't have to create a new model. Howard Gardner had already done it for me. In 1979, as a Harvard researcher, he was asked by a Dutch philanthropic group, the Bernard Van Leer Foundation, to investigate human potential. This invitation led to the founding of Harvard Project Zero, which has served as the institutional midwife for the theory of multiple intelligences. Although Gardner had been thinking about the notion of "many kinds of minds" since at least the mid-1970s (see Gardner 1989, p. 96), the publication in 1983 of his book *Frames of Mind* marked the effective birth date of "MI" theory.

The response to the theory of multiple intelligences was significant. Organizations such as the Rockefeller Foundation, the Lilly Endowment, the Spencer Foundation, and the MacArthur Foundation funded research on the theory. Gardner received recognition for his model from the American Psychological Association, the University of Louisville, and many other groups. Multiple intelligences became a hot topic in the media with reports on *ABC World News Tonight*, *The Today Show*, and *Donahue*, and articles in *Life*, *Newsweek*, *Family Circle*, *The New York Times*, and countless other publications. Around the country, schools began to incorporate multiple intelligences into their programs. The current level of implementation of Gardner's model is hard to gauge, since MI theory is not a fixed program and Gardner has expressed a wish not to person-ally supervise a burgeoning multiple-intelligence empire ("I am not the thought police," he once remarked at an ASCD meeting).

MI theory is perhaps more accurately described as a philosophy of education, an attitude toward learning, or even a meta-model of education in the spirit of John Dewey's ideas on progressive education rather than a set program of fixed techniques and strategies. As such, it offers educators a broad opportunity to creatively adapt its fundamental principles to any number of educational settings. In this volume, I present my own particular adaptation of Gardner's model for teachers. My hope is the book can be used in a number of ways to help stimulate continued reforms in education:

- as a practical introduction to the theory of multiple intelligences for individuals new to the model;
- as a supplementary text for teachers in training in schools of educa-tion;
- as a study guide for groups of teachers and administrators working in schools that are implementing reforms;
- as a resource book for teachers looking for new ideas to enhance their teaching experience.

Each chapter concludes with a section called "For Further Study" that can help readers integrate the material into their instructional practice. Three appendices and a list of references alert readers to other materials related to MI theory that can enrich and extend their understanding of the model.

Many people have helped make this book possible. First, I thank Howard Gardner, whose support of my work over the years has helped fuel my continued involvement in MI theory. I also thank Mert Hanley, director of the Teaching/Learning Center in the West Irondequoit School District in upstate New York, for providing me with the opportunity to work with several school districts in the Rochester area. Over a period of four years in those districts, I tried out many of the ideas in this book. Thanks also to the following individuals who helped in different ways to give form to *Multiple Intelligences in the Classroom:* Sue Teele, David Thornberg, Jo Gusman, Jean Simeone, Pat Kyle, DeLee Lanz, Peggy Buzanski, Dee Dickinson, and my wife, Barbara Turner. Finally, my special appreciation goes to the thousands of teachers, administrators, and students who responded to the ideas and strategies presented in these pages: This book has been created in recognition of the rich potential that exists in each of you.

—Thomas Armstrong

1 The Foundations of the Theory of Multiple Intelligences

It is of the utmost importance that we recognize and nurture all of the varied human intelligences, and all of the combinations of intelligences. We are all so different largely because we all have different combinations of intelligences. If we recognize this, I think we will have at least a better chance of dealing appropriately with the many problems that we face in the world.

—Howard Gardner (1987)

IN 1904, THE MINISTER OF PUBLIC INSTRUCTION in Paris asked the French psychologist Alfred Binet and a group of colleagues to develop a means of determining which primary grade students were "at risk" for failure so these students could receive remedial attention. Out of their efforts came the first intelligence tests. Imported to the United States several years later, intelligence testing became widespread, as did the notion that there was something called "intelligence" that could be objectively measured and reduced to a single number or "IQ" score.

Almost eighty years after the first intelligence tests were developed, a Harvard psychologist named Howard Gardner challenged this commonly held belief. Saying that our culture had defined intelligence too narrowly, he proposed in the book *Frames of Mind* (Gardner 1983) the existence of at least seven basic intelligences. In his theory of multiple intelligences (MI theory), Gardner sought to broaden the scope of human potential beyond the confines of the IQ score. He seriously questioned the validity of determining an individual's intelligence through the practice of taking a person out of his natural learning environment and asking him to do isolated tasks he'd never done before—and probably would never choose to do again. Instead, Gardner suggested that intelligence has more to do

1

with the capacity for (1) solving problems and (2) fashioning products in a context-rich and naturalistic setting.

The Seven Intelligences Described

Once this broader and more pragmatic perspective was taken, the concept of intelligence began to lose its mystique and became a functional concept that could be seen working in people's lives in a variety of ways. Gardner provided a means of mapping the broad range of abilities that humans possess by grouping their capabilities into seven comprehensive categories or "intelligences":

Linguistic Intelligence: The capacity to use words effectively, whether orally (e.g., as a storyteller, orator, or politician) or in writing (e.g., as a poet, playwright, editor, or journalist). This intelligence includes the ability to manipulate the syntax or structure of language, the phonology or sounds of language, the semantics or meanings of language, and the pragmatic dimensions or practical uses of language. Some of these uses include rhetoric (using language to convince others to take a specific course of action), mnemonics (using language to remember information), explanation (using language to inform), and metalanguage (using language to talk about itself).

Logical-Mathematical Intelligence: The capacity to use numbers effectively (e.g., as a mathematician, tax accountant, or statistician) and to reason well (e.g., as a scientist, computer programmer, or logician). This intelligence includes sensitivity to logical patterns and relationships, statements and propositions (if-then, cause-effect), functions, and other related abstractions. The kinds of processes used in the service of logical-mathematical intelligence include: categorization, classification, inference, generalization, calculation, and hypothesis testing.

Spatial Intelligence: The ability to perceive the visual-spatial world accurately (e.g., as a hunter, scout, or guide) and to perform transformations upon those perceptions (e.g., as an interior decorator, architect, artist, or inventor). This intelligence involves sensitivity to color, line, shape, form, space, and the relationships that exist between these elements. It includes the capacity to visualize, to graphically represent visual or spatial ideas, and to orient oneself appropriately in a spatial matrix.

Bodily-Kinesthetic Intelligence: Expertise in using one's whole body to express ideas and feelings (e.g., as an actor, a mime, an athlete, or a dancer) and facility in using one's hands to produce or transform things (e.g., as a craftsperson, sculptor, mechanic, or surgeon). This intelligence includes specific physical skills such as coordination, balance, dexterity, strength, flexibility, and speed, as well as proprioceptive, tactile, and haptic capacities.

Musical Intelligence: The capacity to perceive (e.g., as a music aficionado), discriminate (e.g., as a music critic), transform (e.g., as a composer), and express (e.g., as a performer) musical forms. This intelligence includes sensitivity to the rhythm, pitch or melody, and timbre or tone color of a musical piece. One can have a figural or "top-down" understanding of music (global, intuitive), a formal or "bottom-up" understanding (analytic, technical), or both.

Interpersonal Intelligence: The ability to perceive and make distinctions in the moods, intentions, motivations, and feelings of other people. This can include sensitivity to facial expressions, voice, and gestures; the capacity for discriminating among many different kinds of interpersonal cues; and the ability to respond effectively to those cues in some pragmatic way (e.g., to influence a group of people to follow a certain line of action).

Intrapersonal Intelligence: Self-knowledge and the ability to act adaptively on the basis of that knowledge. This intelligence includes having an accurate picture of oneself (one's strengths and limitations); awareness of inner moods, intentions, motivations, temperaments, and desires; and the capacity for self-discipline, self-understanding, and self-esteem.

The Theoretical Basis for MI Theory

Many people look at the above categories—particularly musical, spatial, and bodily-kinesthetic—and wonder why Howard Gardner insists on calling them intelligences, and not *talents* or *aptitudes*. Gardner realized that people are used to hearing expressions like "He's not very intelligent, but he has a wonderful aptitude for music"; thus, he was quite conscious of his use of the word *intelligence* to describe each category. He said in an interview, "I'm deliberately being somewhat provocative. If I'd said that there's seven kinds of competencies, people would yawn and say 'Yeah, yeah.' But by calling them 'intelligences,' I'm saying that we've tended to put on a pedestal one variety called intelligence, and there's actually a plurality of them, and some are things we've never thought about as being 'intelligence' at all" (Weinreich-Haste 1985, p. 48). To provide a sound theoretical foundation for his claims, Gardner set up certain basic "tests" that each intelligence had to meet to be considered a full-fledged intelligence and not simply a talent, skill, or aptitude. The criteria he used include the following eight factors:

Potential Isolation by Brain Damage. Through his work at the Boston Veterans Administration, Gardner worked with individuals who had suffered accidents or illnesses that affected specific areas of the brain. In several cases, brain lesions seemed to have selectively impaired one intelligence while leaving all the other intelligences intact. For example, a person with a lesion in Broca's area (left frontal lobe) might have a substantial portion of his linguistic intelligence damaged, and thus experience great difficulty speaking, reading, and writing. Yet he might still be able to sing, do math, dance, reflect on feelings, and relate to others. A person with a lesion in the temporal lobe of the right hemisphere might have her musical capacities selectively impaired, while frontal lobe lesions might primarily affect the personal intelligences.

Gardner, then, is arguing for the existence of seven relatively autonomous brain systems—a more sophisticated and updated version of the "right-brain/left-brain" model of learning that was popular in the 1970s. Figure 1.1 on page 7 shows the brain structures for each intelligence.

The Existence of Savants, Prodigies, and Other Exceptional Individuals. Gardner suggests that in some people we can see single intelligences operating at high levels, much like huge mountains rising up against the backdrop of a flat horizon. Savants are individuals who demonstrate superior abilities in part of one intelligence while their other intelligences function at a low level. They seem to exist for each of the seven intelligences. For instance, in the movie *Rain Man* (which is based on a true story), Dustin Hoffman plays the role of Raymond, a logical-mathematical savant. Raymond rapidly calculates multidigit numbers in his head and does other amazing mathematical feats, yet he has poor peer relationships, low language functioning, and a lack of insight into his own life. There are also savants who draw exceptionally well, savants who have amazing musical memories (e.g., playing a composition after hearing it only one time), and savants who read complex material yet don't comprehend what they're reading (hyperlexics).

A Distinctive Developmental History and a Definable Set of Expert "End-State" Performances. Gardner suggests that intelligences are galvanized by participation in some kind of culturally valued activity and that the individual's growth in such an activity follows a developmental pattern. Each intelligence-based activity has its own developmental trajectory; that is, each activity has its own time of arising in early childhood, its own time of peaking during one's lifetime, and its own pattern of either rapidly or gradually declining as one gets older. Musical composition, for example, seems to be among the earliest culturally valued activities to develop to a high level of proficiency: Mozart was only four when he began to compose. Numerous composers and performers have been active well into their eighties and nineties, so expertise in musical composition also seems to remain relatively robust into old age.

Higher mathematical expertise, on the other hand, appears to have a somewhat different trajectory. It doesn't emerge as early as music composition ability (four-year-olds are still working quite concretely with logical ideas), but it does *peak* relatively early in life. Many great mathematical and scientific ideas were developed by teenagers such as Blaise Pascal and Karl Friedrich Gauss. In fact, a review of the history of mathematical ideas suggests that few original mathematical insights come to people past the age of forty. Once people reach this age, they're considered over-the-hill as higher mathematicians! Most of us can breathe a sigh of relief, however, because this decline generally does not seem to affect more pragmatic skills such as balancing a checkbook.

On the other hand, one can become a successful novelist at age forty, fifty, or even later. One can even be over seventy-five and choose to become a painter: Grandma Moses did. Gardner points out that we need to use several different developmental maps in order to understand the seven intelligences. Piaget provides a comprehensive map for logical-mathematical intelligence, but we may need to go to Erik Erikson for a map of the development of the personal intelligences, and to Noam Chomsky or Lev Vygotsky for developmental models of linguistic intelligence. Figure 1.1 includes a summary of developmental trajectories for each intelligence.

FIGURE 1.1

MI Theory Summary Chart

Intelligence	Core Components	Symbol Systems	High End-States
Linguistic	Sensitivity to the sounds, structure, meanings, and functions of words and language	Phonetic languages (e.g., English)	Writer, orator (e.g., Virginia Woolf, Martin Luther King, Jr.)
Logical-Mathematical	Sensitivity to, and capacity to discern, logical or numerical patterns; ability to handle long chains of reasoning	Computer languages (e.g., Pascal)	Scientist, mathematician (e.g., Madame Curie, Blaise Pascal)
Spatial	Capacity to perceive the visual-spatial world accurately and to perform transformations on one's initial perceptions	Ideographic languages (e.g., Chinese)	Artist, architect (e.g., Frida Kahlo, I. M. Pei)
Bodily-Kinesthetic	Ability to control one's body movements and to handle objects skillfully	Sign languages, braille	Athlete, dancer, sculptor (e.g., Jesse Owens, Martha Graham, Auguste Rodin)
Musical	Ability to produce and appreciate rhythm, pitch, and timbre; appreciation of the forms of musical expressiveness	Musical notational systems, Morse Code	Composer, performer (e.g., Stevie Wonder, Midori)
Interpersonal	Capacity to discern and respond appropriately to the moods, temperaments, motivations, and desires of other people	Social cues (e.g., gestures and facial expressions)	Counselor, political leader (e.g., Carl Rogers, Nelson Mandela)
Intrapersonal	Access to one's own feeling life and the ability to discriminate among one's emotions; knowledge of one's own strengths and weaknesses	Symbols of the self (e.g., in dreams and artwork)	Psychotherapist, religious leader (e.g., Sigmund Freud, the Buddha)

continued

Intelligence	Neurological Systems (Primary Areas)	Developmental Factors	Ways That Cultures Value
Linguistic	Left temporal and frontal lobes (e.g., Broca's/Wernicke's areas)	"Explodes" in early childhood; remains robust until old age	oral histories, storytelling, literature, etc.
Logical-Mathematical	Left parietal lobes, right hemisphere	Peaks in adolescence and early adulthood; higher math insights decline after age 40	scientific discoveries, mathematical theories, counting and classification systems, etc.
Spatial	Posterior regions of right hemisphere	Topological thinking in early childhood gives way to Euclidean paradigm around age 9–10; artistic eye stays robust into old age	artistic works, navigational systems, architectural designs inventions, etc.
Bodily-Kinesthetic	Cerebellum, basal ganglia, motor cortex	Varies depending upon component (strength, flexibility, etc.) or domain (gymnastics, baseball, mime, etc.)	crafts, athletic performances, dramatic works, dance forms, sculpture, etc.
Musical	Right temporal lobe	Earliest intelligence to develop; prodigies often go through developmental crisis	musical compositions, performances, recordings, etc.
Interpersonal	Frontal lobes, temporal lobe (esp. right hemisphere), limbic system	Attachment/bonding during first 3 years critical	political documents, social institutions, etc.
Intrapersonal	Frontal lobes, parietal lobes, limbic system	Formation of boundary between self and other during first 3 years critical	religious systems, psychological theories, rites of passage, etc.

continued

8

FIGURE 1.1 (CONTINUED)

Intelligence	Evolutionary Origins	Presence in Other Species	Historical Factors (relative to U.S. in 1990s)
Linguistic	Written notations found dating to 30,000 years ago	Apes' ability to name	Oral transmission more important before printing press
Logical-Mathematical	Early number systems and calendars found	Bees calculate distances through their dances	More important with influence of computers
Spatial	Cave drawings	Territoriality instinct of several species	More important with advent of video and other visual technologies
Bodily-Kinesthetic	Evidence of early tool use	Tool use of primates, anteaters, and other species	Was more important in agrarian period
Musical	Evidence of musical instruments back to Stone Age	Bird song	Was more important during oral culture, when communication was more musical in nature
Interpersonal	Communal living groups required for hunting/gathering	Maternal bonding observed in primates and other species	More important with increase in service economy
Intrapersonal	Early evidence of religious life	Chimpanzees can locate self in mirror; apes experience fear	Continues to be important with increasingly complex society requiring ability to make choices

Finally, Gardner (1993b) points out that we can best see the intelligences working at their zenith by studying the "end-states" of intelligences in the lives of truly exceptional individuals. For example, we can see musical intelligence at work by studying Beethoven's *Eroica* Symphony. Figure 1.1 includes examples of end-states for each intelligence.

An Evolutionary History and Evolutionary Plausibility. Gardner concludes that each of the seven intelligences meets the test of having its roots deeply embedded in the evolution of human beings and, even earlier, in the evolution of other species. So, for example, spatial intelligence can be studied in the cave drawings of Lascaux, as well as in the way certain insects orient themselves in space while tracking flowers. Similarly, musical intelligence can be traced back to archaeological evidence of early musical instruments, as well as through the wide variety of bird songs. Figure 1.1 includes notes on the evolutionary origins of the intelligences.

MI theory also has a historical context. Certain intelligences seem to have been more important in earlier times than they are today. Bodily-kinesthetic intelligence, for example, was valued more a hundred years ago in the United States, when a majority of the population lived in rural settings and the ability to harvest grain and build silos had strong social approbation. Similarly, certain intelligences may become more important in the future. As a greater percentage of the citizenry receive their information from films, television, videotapes, and CD-ROM technology, the value placed on having a strong spatial intelligence may increase. Figure 1.1 notes some of the historical factors that have influenced the perceived value of each intelligence.

Support from Psychometric Findings. Standardized measures of human ability provide the "test" that most theories of intelligence (as well as many learning-style theories) use to ascertain the validity of a model. Although Gardner is no champion of standardized tests, and in fact has been an ardent supporter of alternatives to formal testing (see Chapter 10), he suggests that we can look at many existing standardized tests for support of the theory of multiple intelligences (although Gardner would point out that standardized tests assess multiple intelligences in a strikingly decontextualized fashion). For example, the Wechsler Intelligence Scale for Children includes sub-tests that require linguistic intelligence (e.g., information, vocabulary), logical-mathematical intelligence (e.g., arithmetic), spatial intelligence (e.g., picture arrangement), and to a lesser extent bodily-kinesthetic intelligence (e.g., object assembly). Still other assessments tap personal intelligences (e.g., the Vineland Society Maturity Scale and the Coopersmith Self-Esteem Inventory). Chapter 3 includes a survey of the types of formal tests associated with each of the seven intelligences.

Support from Experimental Psychological Tasks. Gardner suggests that by looking at specific psychological studies, we can witness intelligences working in isolation from one another. For example, in studies where subjects master a specific skill, such as reading, but fail to transfer that ability to another area, such as mathematics, we see the failure of linguistic ability to transfer to logical-mathematical intelligence. Similarly, in studies of cognitive abilities such as memory, perception, or attention, we can see evidence that individuals possess selective abilities. Certain individuals, for instance, may have a superior memory for words but not for faces; others may have acute perception of musical sounds but not verbal sounds. Each of these cognitive faculties, then, is intelligence-specific; that is, people can demonstrate different levels of proficiency across the seven intelligences in each cognitive area.

An Identifiable Core Operation or Set of Operations. Gardner says that much as a computer program requires a set of operations (e.g., DOS) in order for it to function, each intelligence has a set of core operations that serve to drive the various activities indigenous to that intelligence. In musical intelligence, e.g., those components may include sensitivity to pitch or the ability to discriminate among various rhythmic structures. In bodily-kinesthetic intelligence, core operations may include the ability to imitate the physical movements of others or the capacity to master established fine-motor routines for building a structure. Gardner speculates that these core operations may someday be identified with such precision as to be simulated on a computer.

Susceptibility to Encoding in a Symbol System. One of the best indicators of intelligent behavior, according to Gardner, is the capacity of human beings to use symbols. The word "cat" that appears here on the page is simply a collection of marks printed in a specific way. Yet it probably conjures up for you an entire range of associations, images, and memories. What has occurred is the bringing to the present ("re-presentation") of something that is not actually here. Gardner suggests that the ability to symbolize is one of the most important factors separating humans from most other species. He notes that each of the seven intelligences in his theory meets the criterion of being able to be symbolized. Each intelligence, in fact, has its own unique symbol or notational systems. For linguistic intelligence, there are a number of spoken and written languages such as English, French, and Spanish. Spatial intelligence, on the other hand, includes a range of graphic languages used by architects, engineers, and designers, as well as certain ideographic languages such as Chinese. Figure 1.1 includes examples of symbol systems for all seven intelligences.

Key Points In MI Theory

Beyond the descriptions of the seven intelligences and their theoretical underpinnings, certain points of the model are important to remember:

1. Each person possesses all seven intelligences. MI theory is not a "type theory" for determining the *one* intelligence that fits. It is a theory of cognitive functioning, and it proposes that each person has capacities in all seven intelligences. Of course, the seven intelligences function together in ways unique to each person. Some people appear to possess extremely high levels of functioning in all or most of the seven intelligences—for example, German poet-statesman-scientist-philosopher Johann Wolfgang von Goethe. Other people, such as those in institutions for the developmentally disabled, appear to lack all but the most rudimentary aspects of the intelligences. Most of us fall somewhere in between these two poles—being highly developed in some intelligences, modestly developed in others, and relatively underdeveloped in the rest.

2. Most people can develop each intelligence to an adequate level of competency. Although an individual may bewail his deficiencies in a given area and consider his problems innate and intractable, Gardner suggests that virtually everyone has the capacity to develop all seven intelligences to a reasonably high level of performance if given the appropriate encouragement, enrichment, and instruction. He points to the Suzuki Talent Education Program as an example of how individuals of relatively modest biological musical endowment can achieve a sophisticated level of proficiency in playing the violin or piano through a combination of the right environmental influences (for example, an involved parent, exposure from infancy to classical music, and early instruction). Such educational models can be found in other intelligences as well (see, for example, Edwards 1979).

3. Intelligences usually work together in complex ways. Gardner points out that each intelligence as described above is actually a "fiction"; that is, no intelligence exists by itself in life (except perhaps in very rare instances in savants and brain-injured individuals). Intelligences are always interacting with each other. To cook a meal, one must read the recipe (linguistic), possibly divide the recipe in half (logical-mathematical), develop a menu that satisfies all members of a family (interpersonal), and placate one's own appetite as well (intrapersonal). Similarly, when a child plays a game of kickball, he needs bodily-kinesthetic intelligence (to run, kick, and catch), spatial intelligence (to orient himself to the playing field and to anticipate the trajectories of flying balls), and linguistic and interpersonal intelligences (to successfully argue a point during a dispute in the game). The intelligences have been taken out of context in MI theory only for the purpose of examining their essential features and learning how to use them effectively. We must always remember to put them back into their specific culturally valued contexts when we are finished with their formal study.

4. There are many ways to be intelligent within each category. There is no standard set of attributes that one must have to be considered intelligent in a specific area. Consequently, a person may not be able to read, yet be highly linguistic because he can tell a terrific story or has a large oral vocabulary. Similarly, a person may be quite awkward on the playing field, yet possess superior bodily-kinesthetic intelligence when she weaves a carpet or creates an inlaid chess table. MI theory emphasizes the rich diversity of ways in which people show their gifts *within* intelligences as well as *between* intelligences. (See Chapter 3 for more information on the varieties of attributes in each intelligence.)

The Existence of Other Intelligences

Gardner points out that his model of seven intelligences is a tentative formulation; after further research and investigation, some of the intelligences on his list may not meet certain of the eight criteria described above, and therefore no longer qualify as intelligences. On the other hand, we may identify *new* intelligences that do meet the various tests. Other intelligences that have been proposed include:

- spirituality
- moral sensibility
- sexuality
- humor
- intuition
- creativity
- culinary (cooking) ability
- olfactory perception (sense of smell)
- an ability to synthesize the other intelligences

It remains to be seen, however, whether these proposed intelligences can, in fact, meet each of the eight tests described above.

The Relationship of MI Theory to Other Intelligence Theories

Gardner's theory of multiple intelligences is certainly not the first model to grapple with the notion of intelligence. There have been theories of intelligence since ancient times, when the mind was considered to reside somewhere in the heart, the liver, or the kidneys. In more recent times, theories of intelligence have emerged touting anywhere from 1 (Spearman's "g") to 150 (Guilford's Structure of the Intellect) types of intelligence.

A growing number of learning-style theories also deserve to be mentioned here. Broadly construed, a person's learning style is *the intelligences put to work.* In other words, learning styles are the pragmatic manifestations of intelligences operating in natural learning contexts. For example, a child with a highly developed spatial intelligence may show a preference for, and a superiority in, learning about new things through pictures, drawing activities, three-dimensional building materials, videotapes, and computer programs containing graphics. (See Chapter 3 for more information on identifying children's intellectual proclivities.)

How, then, does MI theory fit in with the many learning-style theories that have gained adherents over the past two decades? To relate MI theory to other models is a tempting project, since learners expand their knowledge base by linking new information (in this case, MI theory) to existing schemes or models (the learning-style model they're most familiar with). This task is not so easy an undertaking, however, partly because MI theory has a different type of underlying structure than many of the most current learning-style theories. MI theory is a *cognitive* model that seeks to describe how individuals use their intelligences to solve problems and fashion products. Unlike other models that are primarily process oriented, Gardner's approach is particularly geared to how the human mind operates on the *contents* of the world (e.g., objects, persons, certain types of sounds, etc.). A seemingly related theory, the Visual-Auditory-Kinesthetic model, is actually very different from MI theory, in that it is a *sensory-channel* model (MI theory is not specifically tied to the senses; it is possible to be blind and have spatial intelligence or to be deaf and be quite musical). Another popular theory, the Myers-Briggs model, is actually a *personality* theory based on Carl Jung's theoretical formulation of different types of personalities. To attempt to correlate MI theory with models like these is akin to comparing apples with oranges. Although we can identify relationships and connections, our efforts may resemble those of the Blind Men and the Elephant: each model touching upon a different aspect of the whole learner.

For Further Study

In this chapter, I have presented the basic tenets of the theory of multiple intelligences in a brief and concise way. MI theory has connections with a wide range of fields, including anthropology, cognitive psychology, developmental psychology, studies of exceptional individuals, psychometrics, and neuropsychology. There is ample opportunity to explore the theory in its own right, quite apart from its specific educational uses. Such a preliminary study may actually help you apply the theory in the classroom. Here are some suggestions for exploring more deeply the foundations of MI theory.

1. Form a study group on MI theory using Howard Gardner's seminal book *Frames of Mind: The Theory of Multiple Intelligences* (New York: Basic Books, 1983) as a text. Each member can be responsible for reading and reporting on a specific chapter.

2. Use Gardner's exhaustive bibliography on MI theory found in his book *Multiple Intelligences: The Theory in Practice* (New York: Basic Books, 1993a) as a basis for reading more widely on the model.

3. Propose the existence of a new intelligence and apply Gardner's eight criteria to see if it qualifies for inclusion in MI theory.

4. Collect examples of symbol systems in each intelligence. For instance, see Robert McKim's book *Experiences in Visual Thinking* (Boston: PWS Engineering, 1980) for examples of several spatial "languages" used by designers, architects, artists, and inventors.

5. Read about savants in each intelligence. Some of the footnoted entries in Gardner's *Frames of Mind* identify sources of information on savants in logical-mathematical, spatial, musical, linguistic, and bodily-kinesthetic intelligences.

6. Relate MI theory to a current learning-style model.

2 MI and Personal Development

> What kind of school plan you make is neither here nor there; what matters is what sort of a person you are.
>
> —Rudolf Steiner (1964)

BEFORE APPLYING ANY MODEL OF LEARNING in a classroom environment, we should first apply it to ourselves as educators and adult learners, for unless we have an experiential understanding of the theory and have personalized its content, we are unlikely to be committed to using it with students. Consequently, an important step in using the theory of multiple intelligences (after grasping the basic theoretical foundations presented in Chapter 1) is to determine the nature and quality of our *own* multiple intelligences and seek ways to develop them in our lives. As we begin to do this, it will become apparent how our particular fluency (or lack of fluency) in each of the seven intelligences affects our competence (or lack of competence) in the various roles we have as educators.

Identifying Your Multiple Intelligences

As you will see in the later chapters on student assessment (Chapters 3 and 10), developing a profile of a person's multiple intelligences is not a simple matter. No test can accurately determine the nature or quality of a person's intelligences. As Howard Gardner has repeatedly pointed out, standardized tests measure only a small part of the total spectrum of abilities. The best way to assess your own multiple intelligences, therefore, is through a realistic appraisal of your performance in the many kinds of tasks, activities, and experiences associated with each intelligence. Rather than perform several artificial learning tasks, look back over the kinds of

16

real-life experiences you've already had in these seven intelligences. The MI inventory in Figure 2.1 on pages 18–20 can assist you in doing this.

It's important to keep in mind that this inventory is *not* a test, and that quantitative information (such as the number of checks for each intelligence) has no bearing on determining your intelligence or lack of intelligence in each category. The purpose of the inventory is to begin to connect you to your own life experiences with the seven intelligences. What sorts of memories, feelings, and ideas emerge from this process?

Tapping MI Resources

The theory of multiple intelligences is an especially good model for looking at teaching strengths as well as for examining areas needing improvement. Perhaps you avoid drawing pictures on the blackboard or stay away from using highly graphic materials in your presentations because spatial intelligence is not particularly well developed in your life. Or possibly you gravitate toward cooperative learning strategies because you are an interpersonal sort of learner/teacher yourself. Use MI theory to survey your teaching style and see how it matches up with the seven intelligences. While you don't have to be a master in all seven intelligences, you probably should know how to tap resources in the intelligences you typically shy away from in the classroom. Some ways to do this include:

Drawing on Colleagues' Expertise. If you don't have ideas for bringing music into the classroom because your musical intelligence is undeveloped, consider getting help from the school's music teacher or a musically inclined colleague. The theory of multiple intelligences has broad implications for team teaching. In a school committed to developing students' multiple intelligences, the ideal teaching team or curriculum planning committee includes expertise in all seven intelligences; that is, each member possesses a high level of development in a different intelligence.

Asking Students to Help Out. Students can often come up with strategies and demonstrate expertise in areas where teachers may be deficient. For example, students may be able to do some picture drawing on the board or provide musical background for a learning activity if you don't feel comfortable doing these things yourself.

18

FIGURE 2.1
An MI Inventory for Adults

Check those statements that apply in each intelligence category. Space has been provided at the end of each intelligence for you to write additional information not specifically referred to in the inventory items.

Linguistic Intelligence

_____ Books are very important to me.

_____ I can hear words in my head before I read, speak, or write them down.

_____ I get more out of listening to the radio or a spoken-word cassette than I do from television or films.

_____ I enjoy word games like Scrabble, Anagrams, or Password.

_____ I enjoy entertaining myself or others with tongue twisters, nonsense rhymes, or puns.

_____ Other people sometimes have to stop and ask me to explain the meaning of the words I use in my writing and speaking.

_____ English, social studies, and history were easier for me in school than math and science.

_____ When I drive down a freeway, I pay more attention to the words written on billboards than to the scenery.

_____ My conversation includes frequent references to things that I've read or heard.

_____ I've written something recently that I was particularly proud of or that earned me recognition from others.

Other Linguistic Strengths:

Logical-Mathematical Intelligence

_____ I can easily compute numbers in my head.

_____ Math and/or science were among my favorite subjects in school.

_____ I enjoy playing games or solving brainteasers that require logical thinking.

_____ I like to set up little "what if" experiments (for example, "What if I double the amount of water I give to my rosebush each week?")

_____ My mind searches for patterns, regularities, or logical sequences in things.

_____ I'm interested in new developments in science.

_____ I believe that almost everything has a rational explanation.

_____ I sometimes think in clear, abstract, wordless, imageless concepts.

_____ I like finding logical flaws in things that people say and do at home and work.

_____ I feel more comfortable when something has been measured, categorized, analyzed, or quantified in some way.

Other Logical-Mathematical Strengths:

Spatial Intelligence

_____ I often see clear visual images when I close my eyes.

_____ I'm sensitive to color.

_____ I frequently use a camera or camcorder to record what I see around me.
_____ I enjoy doing jigsaw puzzles, mazes, and other visual puzzles.
_____ I have vivid dreams at night.
_____ I can generally find my way around unfamiliar territory.
_____ I like to draw or doodle.
_____ Geometry was easier for me than algebra in school.
_____ I can comfortably imagine how something might appear if it were looked down upon from directly above in a bird's-eye view.
_____ I prefer looking at reading material that is heavily illustrated.

Other Spatial Strengths:

Bodily-Kinesthetic Intelligence
_____ I engage in at least one sport or physical activity on a regular basis.
_____ I find it difficult to sit still for long periods of time.
_____ I like working with my hands at concrete activities such as sewing, weaving, carving, carpentry, or model building.
_____ My best ideas often come to me when I'm out for a long walk or a jog, or when I'm engaging in some other kind of physical activity.
_____ I often like to spend my free time outdoors.
_____ I frequently use hand gestures or other forms of body language when conversing with someone.
_____ I need to touch things in order to learn more about them.
_____ I enjoy daredevil amusement rides or similar thrilling physical experiences.
_____ I would describe myself as well coordinated.
_____ I need to practice a new skill rather than simply reading about it or seeing a video that describes it.

Other Bodily-Kinesthetic Strengths:

Musical Intelligence
_____ I have a pleasant singing voice.
_____ I can tell when a musical note is off-key.
_____ I frequently listen to music on radio, records, cassettes, or compact discs.
_____ I play a musical instrument.
_____ My life would be poorer if there were no music in it.
_____ I sometimes catch myself walking down the street with a television jingle or other tune running through my mind.
_____ I can easily keep time to a piece of music with a simple percussion instrument.
_____ I know the tunes to many different songs or musical pieces.
_____ If I hear a musical selection once or twice, I am usually able to sing it back fairly accurately.
_____ I often make tapping sounds or sing little melodies while working, studying, or learning something new.

Other Musical Strengths:

continued

Interpersonal Intelligence

_____ I'm the sort of person that people come to for advice and counsel at work or in my neighborhood.

_____ I prefer group sports like badminton, volleyball, or softball to solo sports such as swimming and jogging.

_____ When I have a problem, I'm more likely to seek out another person for help than attempt to work it out on my own.

_____ I have at least three close friends.

_____ I favor social pastimes such as Monopoly or bridge over individual recreations such as video games and solitaire.

_____ I enjoy the challenge of teaching another person, or groups of people, what I know how to do.

_____ I consider myself a leader (or others have called me that).

_____ I feel comfortable in the midst of a crowd.

_____ I like to get involved in social activities connected with my work, church, or community.

_____ I would rather spend my evenings at a lively party than stay at home alone.

Other Interpersonal Strengths:

Intrapersonal Intelligence

_____ I regularly spend time alone meditating, reflecting, or thinking about important life questions.

_____ I have attended counseling sessions or personal growth seminars to learn more about myself.

_____ I am able to respond to setbacks with resilience.

_____ I have a special hobby or interest that I keep pretty much to myself.

_____ I have some important goals for my life that I think about on a regular basis.

_____ I have a realistic view of my strengths and weaknesses (borne out by feedback from other sources).

_____ I would prefer to spend a weekend alone in a cabin in the woods rather than at a fancy resort with lots of people around.

_____ I consider myself to be strong willed or independent minded.

_____ I keep a personal diary or journal to record the events of my inner life.

_____ I am self-employed or have at least thought seriously about starting my own business.

Other Intrapersonal Strengths:

Source: From _7 Kinds of Smart_ by Thomas Armstrong. Copyright © 1993 by Thomas Armstrong. Used by permission of Dutton Signet, a division of Penguin Books USA Inc.

Using Available Technology. Tap your school's technical resources to convey information you might not be able to provide yourself. For instance, you can use tape recordings of music if you're not musical, videotapes if you're not picture-oriented, calculators and self-paced computer software to supplement your shortcomings in logical-mathematical areas, and so on.

The final way to come to grips with intelligences that seem to be "blind spots" in your life is through a process of careful cultivation or personal development of your intelligences. MI theory provides a model through which you can activate your neglected intelligences and balance your use of all the intelligences.

Developing Your Multiple Intelligences

I've been careful not to use the terms "strong intelligence" and "weak intelligence" in describing individual differences among a person's intelligences, because a person's "weak" intelligence may actually turn out to be her *strongest* intelligence, once given the chance to develop. As mentioned in Chapter 1, a key point in MI theory is that *most people can develop all their intelligences to a relatively competent level of mastery.* Whether intelligences develop depends on three main factors:

• **Biological endowment**, including hereditary or genetic factors and insults or injuries to the brain before, during, and after birth;

• **Personal life history**, including experiences with parents, teachers, peers, friends, and others who either awaken intelligences or keep them from developing;

• **Cultural and historical background**, including the time and place in which you were born and raised and the nature and state of cultural or historical developments in different domains.

We can see the interaction of these factors in the life of Wolfgang Amadeus Mozart. Mozart undoubtedly came into life already possessing a strong biological endowment (a healthy right temporal lobe perhaps). And he was born into a family of musical individuals; in fact, his father, Leopold, was a composer who gave up his own career to support his son's musical development. Finally, Mozart was born at a time in Europe when the arts (including music) were flourishing and wealthy patrons supported composers and performers. Mozart's genius, therefore, arose through a confluence of biological, personal, and cultural/historical factors. What would have happened, however, if Mozart had instead been born to tone-deaf parents in Puritan England, where most music was considered the devil's work? His musical gifts likely would never have developed to a high level because of the forces working against his biological endowment.

The interaction of the above factors is also evident in the musical proficiency of many of the people who have been enrolled in the Suzuki Talent Education Program. Born with a relatively modest genetic musical endowment, these people have developed their musical intelligence to a high level through experiences in the program. MI theory is a model that values *nurture* as much as, and probably more than, *nature* in accounting for the development of intelligences.

Activators and Deactivators of Intelligences

Crystallizing experiences and *paralyzing experiences* are two key processes in the development of intelligences. Crystallizing experiences, a concept originating with David Feldman (1980) at Tufts University and further developed by Howard Gardner and his colleagues (see Walters and Gardner 1986), are the "turning points" in the development of a person's talents and abilities. Often these events occur in early childhood, although they can occur anytime during the life span. For instance, when Albert Einstein was four years old, his father showed him a magnetic compass. The adult Einstein later said this compass filled him with a desire to ferret out the mysteries of the universe. Essentially, this experience activated his sleeping genius and started him on his journey toward discoveries that would make him one of the towering figures in 20th century thought. Similarly, when Yehudi Menuhin was almost four, his parents took him to a concert by the San Francisco Symphony Orchestra. The experience so enthralled him that afterwards he asked his parents for a violin as a birthday present, and he said he wanted the violin soloist they heard that evening to teach him to play it! Crystallizing experiences, then, are the sparks that light an intelligence and start its development toward maturity.

Conversely, I use the term *paralyzing experiences* to refer to experiences that "shut down" intelligences. Perhaps a teacher humiliated you in front of your classmates when you showed your latest artistic creation during art period, and that event marked the end of a good part of your spatial development. Possibly a parent yelled at you to "stop making a racket" on the piano, and you never went near a musical instrument after that. Paralyzing experiences are often filled with shame, guilt, fear, anger, and other negative emotions that prevent our intelligences from growing and thriving (see Miller 1981).

A number of other environmental influences also promote or retard the development of intelligences. They include:

• **Access to resources or mentors:** If your family was so poor that you couldn't afford a violin, piano, or other instrument, your musical intelligence might well have remained undeveloped.

• **Historical-cultural factors:** If you were a student who demonstrated "proclivities" in mathematics at a time when math and science programs were highly funded, your logical-mathematical intelligence would likely have developed.

• **Geographic factors:** If you grew up on a farm, you might well have had more opportunity to develop certain aspects of bodily-kinesthetic intelligence than if you were raised on the 62nd floor of a Manhattan high-rise apartment.

• **Familial factors:** If you wanted to be an artist but your parents wanted you to be a lawyer, their influence might well have promoted the development of your linguistic intelligence at the expense of your spatial intelligence.

• **Situational factors:** If you had to help take care of a large family while you were growing up, and you now have a large family yourself, you may have had little time to develop in areas of promise—unless they were interpersonal in nature.

MI theory offers a model of personal development that can help educators understand how their own learning style (profile of intelligences) affects their teaching style in the classroom. Further, it opens the gate to a broad range of activities that can help us develop neglected intelligences, activate underdeveloped or paralyzed intelligences, and bring well-developed intelligences to even higher levels of proficiency.

For Further Study

1. Fill out the inventory in this chapter. Talk with a friend or colleague about the results of the inventory. Make sure to share something about what you perceive as your most developed intelligences and your least developed intelligences. Avoid talking in terms of quantitative information ("I had only three checks in musical intelligence"). Speak instead in anecdotal terms: "I've never felt very musical in my life; my classmates used to laugh at me when I had to sing solo in music class."

Also, begin to reflect upon how your developed and undeveloped intelligences affect what you put into, or keep out of, your work as an educator. What kinds of teaching methods or materials do you avoid because they involve using your underdeveloped intelligences? What sorts of things are you especially good at doing because of one or more highly developed intelligences?

2. Select an intelligence that you would like to nurture. It may be an intelligence you showed particular promise in as a child but never had the opportunity to develop (the intelligence may have gone "underground" as you grew up). Or perhaps it is an intelligence you have had great difficulty with and that you want to experience more competence and confidence in. Or, possibly, it's a highly developed intelligence that you want to take to an even higher level. Using a piece of mural paper perhaps five feet in length, create a time line showing the development of that intelligence from early childhood to the present. Note significant events along the way, including crystallizing and paralyzing experiences, people who helped you develop the intelligence (or sought to suppress it), school influences, what happened to the intelligence as you became an adult, and so forth. Leave space on the time line to include information about the *future* development of the intelligence (see Study Item 4 below).

3. Create a curriculum planning team or other school group that consists of individuals representing each of the seven intelligences. Before beginning the planning work, take time to share your personal experiences of your most highly developed intelligence.

4. Select an intelligence that is not very highly developed in your life and create a plan for cultivating it. Look over suggestions for developing the intelligences in *7 Kinds of Smart* (Armstrong 1993), or create your own list of ways to nurture each intelligence. As you begin personally developing an intelligence, notice whether this process influences what you do in the classroom. Are you bringing more aspects of that intelligence into your professional work?

3 Describing Intelligences in Students

ALTHOUGH IT'S TRUE THAT EACH CHILD possesses all seven intelligences and can develop all seven to a fairly high level of competence, children seem to begin showing what Howard Gardner calls "proclivities" (or inclinations) in specific intelligences from a very early age. By the time children begin school, they have probably established ways of learning that run more along the lines of some intelligences than others. In this chapter, we will examine how you can begin to describe students' most developed intelligences so that more of their learning in school can take place through their preferred intelligences.

Figure 3.1 provides brief descriptions of the learning styles of children who display proclivities in specific intelligences. Keep in mind, however, that most students have strengths in *several* areas, so you should avoid pigeonholing a child in one intelligence. You will probably find each student pictured in at least two or three of these intelligence descriptions.

Assessing Students' Multiple Intelligences

There is no "mega-test" on the market that can provide a comprehensive survey of your students' multiple intelligences. If anyone should tell you they have a computer-scored test that in fifteen minutes can provide a bar graph showing the seven "peaks" and "valleys" of each student in your class or school, I'd suggest that you be very skeptical. This isn't to say that formal testing can't provide some information about a student's

FIGURE 3.1
Seven Kinds of Learning Styles

Children who are strongly:	Think	Love	Need
Linguistic	in words	reading, writing, telling stories, playing word games, etc.	books, tapes, writing tools, paper, diaries, dialogue, discussion, debate, stories, etc.
Logical-Mathematical	by reasoning	experimenting, questioning, figuring out logical puzzles, calculating, etc.	things to explore and think about, science materials, manipulatives, trips to the planetarium and science museum, etc.
Spatial	in images and pictures	designing, drawing, visualizing, doodling, etc.	art, LEGOs, video, movies, slides, imagination games, mazes, puzzles, illustrated books, trips to art museums, etc.
Bodily-Kinesthetic	through somatic sensations	dancing, running, jumping, building, touching, gesturing, etc.	role play, drama, movement, things to build, sports and physical games, tactile experiences, hands-on learning, etc.
Musical	via rhythms and melodies	singing, whistling, humming, tapping feet and hands, listening, etc.	sing-along time, trips to concerts, music playing at home and school, musical instruments, etc.
Interpersonal	by bouncing ideas off other people	leading, organizing, relating, manipulating, mediating, partying, etc.	friends, group games, social gatherings, community events, clubs, mentors/apprenticeships, etc.
Intrapersonal	deeply inside of themselves	setting goals, meditating, dreaming, being quiet, planning	secret places, time alone, self-paced projects, choices, etc.

intelligences; as I discuss later, it can provide clues to various intelligences. The single best tool for assessing students' multiple intelligences, however, is probably one readily available to all of us: simple observation.

I've often humorously suggested to teachers that one good way to identify students' most highly developed intelligences is to observe how they *misbehave* in class. The strongly linguistic student will be talking out of turn, the highly spatial student will be doodling and daydreaming, the interpersonally inclined student will be socializing, the bodily-kinesthetic student will be fidgeting, and so forth. These students are metaphorically saying through their misbehaviors: "This is how I learn, teacher, and if you don't teach me through my most natural learning channels, guess what? I'm going to do it *anyway.*" These intelligence-specific misbehaviors, then, are a sort of cry for help—a diagnostic indicator of how students need to be taught.

Another good observational indicator of students' proclivities is how they spend their free time in school. In other words, what do they do when nobody is telling them what to do? If you have a "choice time" in class when students can choose from a number of activities, what activities do students pick? Highly linguistic students might gravitate toward books, social students toward group games and gossip, spatial students towards drawing, and bodily-kinesthetic students towards hands-on building activities. Observing kids in these student-initiated activities can tell a world about how they learn most effectively.

Every teacher should consider keeping a notebook, diary, or journal handy in a desk or on a shelf for recording observations of this kind. Of course, if you're working with 150 students a day at the middle school or high school level, regular recording of observations for each student would hardly be possible. You might, however, single out the two or three most troublesome or puzzling students in class, and focus your MI assessment upon them. Even if you have a class of 25 to 35 students, writing a couple of lines about each student each week may pay off in the long run. Writing two lines a week for forty weeks yields eighty lines, or three to four pages of solid observational data for each student.

To help organize your observations of a student's multiple intelligences, you can use a checklist like the one in Figure 3.2. Keep in mind that this checklist is not a test and should only be used in conjunction with other sources of assessment information when describing students' multiple intelligences.

FIGURE 3.2

Checklist for Assessing Students' Multiple Intelligences

Name of Student: _____

Check items that apply:

Linguistic Intelligence

_____ writes better than average for age
_____ spins tall tales or tells jokes and stories
_____ has a good memory for names, places, dates, or trivia
_____ enjoys word games
_____ enjoys reading books
_____ spells words accurately (or if preschool, does developmental spelling that is advanced for age)
_____ appreciates nonsense rhymes, puns, tongue twisters, etc.
_____ enjoys listening to the spoken word (stories, commentary on the radio, talking books, etc.)
_____ has a good vocabulary for age
_____ communicates to others in a highly verbal way

Other Linguistic Strengths:

Logical-Mathematical Intelligence

_____ asks a lot of questions about how things work
_____ computes arithmetic problems in his/her head quickly (or if preschool, math concepts are advanced for age)
_____ enjoys math class (or if preschool, enjoys counting and doing other things with numbers)
_____ finds math computer games interesting (or if no exposure to computers, enjoys other math or counting games)
_____ enjoys playing chess, checkers, or other strategy games (or if preschool, board games requiring counting squares)
_____ enjoys working on logic puzzles or brainteasers (or if preschool, enjoys hearing logical nonsense such as in *Alice's Adventures in Wonderland*)
_____ enjoys putting things in categories or hierarchies
_____ likes to experiment in a way that shows higher order cognitive thinking processes
_____ thinks on a more abstract or conceptual level than peers
_____ has a good sense of cause-effect for age

Other Logical-Mathematical Strengths:

continued

Spatial Intelligence
_____ reports clear visual images
_____ reads maps, charts, and diagrams more easily than text (or if preschool, enjoys looking at more than text)
_____ daydreams more than peers
_____ enjoys art activities
_____ draws figures that are advanced for age
_____ likes to view movies, slides, or other visual presentations
_____ enjoys doing puzzles, mazes, "Where's Waldo?" or similar visual activities
_____ builds interesting three-dimensional constructions for age (e.g., LEGO buildings)
_____ gets more out of pictures than words while reading
_____ doodles on workbooks, worksheets, or other materials

Other Spatial Strengths:

Bodily-Kinesthetic Intelligence
_____ excels in one or more sports (or if preschool, shows physical prowess advanced for age)
_____ moves, twitches, taps, or fidgets while seated for a long time in one spot
_____ cleverly mimics other people's gestures or mannerisms
_____ loves to take things apart and put them back together again
_____ puts his/her hands all over something he/she's just seen
_____ enjoys running, jumping, wrestling, or similar activities (or if older, will show these interests in a more "restrained" way—e.g., punching a friend, running to class, jumping over a chair)
_____ shows skill in a craft (e.g., woodworking, sewing, mechanics) or good fine-motor coordination in other ways
_____ has a dramatic way of expressing herself/himself
_____ reports different physical sensations while thinking or working
_____ enjoys working with clay or other tactile experiences (e.g., fingerpainting)

Other Bodily-Kinesthetic Strengths:

Musical Intelligence
_____ tells you when music sounds off-key or disturbing in some other way
_____ remembers melodies of songs
_____ has a good singing voice
_____ plays a musical instrument or sings in a choir or other group (or if preschool, enjoys playing percussion instruments and/or singing in a group)
_____ has a rhythmic way of speaking and/or moving
_____ unconsciously hums to himself/herself
_____ taps rhythmically on the table or desk as he/she works
_____ sensitive to environmental noises (e.g., rain on the roof)

_____ responds favorably when a piece of music is put on
_____ sings songs that he/she has learned outside of the classroom

Other Musical Strengths:

Interpersonal Intelligence
_____ enjoys socializing with peers
_____ seems to be a natural leader
_____ gives advice to friends who have problems
_____ seems to be street-smart
_____ belongs to clubs, committees, or other organizations (or if preschool, seems to be part of a regular social group)
_____ enjoys informally teaching other kids
_____ likes to play games with other kids
_____ has two or more close friends
_____ has a good sense of empathy or concern for others
_____ others seek out his/her company

Other Interpersonal Strengths:

Intrapersonal Intelligence
_____ displays a sense of independence or a strong will
_____ has a realistic sense of his/her strengths and weaknesses
_____ does well when left alone to play or study
_____ marches to the beat of a different drummer in his/her style of living and learning
_____ has an interest or hobby that he/she doesn't talk much about
_____ has a good sense of self-direction
_____ prefers working alone to working with others
_____ accurately expresses how he/she is feeling
_____ is able to learn from his/her failures and successes in life
_____ has high self-esteem.

Other Intrapersonal Strengths:

In addition to observation and checklists, there are several other excellent ways to get assessment information about students' multiple intelligences:

Collect Documents. Anecdotal records are not the only way to document students' strongest intelligences. Teachers should consider having a Polaroid camera available to snap pictures of students displaying evidence of their multiple intelligences. Photographs are particularly useful for documenting products that might be gone in another ten minutes, like giant LEGO structures. If students show a particular capacity for telling stories or singing songs, record them and keep the cassette as a document. If students have drawing or painting abilities, keep samples of their work or take photographs or slides of it. If students show their greatest assets during a football game or through a hands-on demonstration of how to fix a machine, capture their performance on videotape. Ultimately, MI assessment data will consist of several kinds of documents, including photos, sketches, samples of school work, audio cassettes, videotapes, color photocopies, and more. The use of CD-ROM technology and hypertext formats may allow all of this information to be conveniently included on a single disc and reviewed by teachers, administrators, parents, and students themselves. (For more on assessment through multiple intelligences, see Chapter 10).

Look at School Records. Cumulative records, as two-dimensional and lifeless as they sometimes appear, can provide important information about a student's multiple intelligences. Look at the student's grades over the years. Are grades in math and the hard sciences consistently higher than grades in literature and the social sciences? If so, this is evidence of an inclination toward logical-mathematical over linguistic intelligence. High art and drafting grades may indicate well-developed spatial intelligence, while A's and B's in PE and shop class may point toward bodily-kinesthetic abilities. Similarly, test scores can sometimes provide differential information about a student's intelligences. On intelligence tests, for example, there are often sub-tests that tap linguistic intelligence (vocabulary and "information" categories), logical-mathematical intelligence (analogies, arithmetic), and spatial intelligence (picture arrangement, block design, etc.). A number of other tests may point toward specific intelligences. Here is a partial list of the kinds of tests that may relate to each intelligence:

- *Linguistic:* reading tests, language tests, the verbal sections of intelligence and achievement tests
- *Logical-Mathematical:* Piagetian assessments, math achievement tests, the reasoning sections of intelligence tests
- *Spatial:* visual memory and visual-motor tests, art aptitude tests, some performance items on intelligence tests
- *Bodily-Kinesthetic:* sensory-motor tests, some motor sub-tests in neuropsychological batteries, the Presidential physical fitness test
- *Interpersonal:* social maturity scales, sociograms, interpersonal projective tests (e.g., Family Kinetic Drawing)
- *Intrapersonal:* self-concept assessments, projective tests

School records may also contain valuable anecdotal information about a student's multiple intelligences. One of the most valuable sources, I've discovered, is the kindergarten teacher's report. Often, the kindergarten teacher is the only educator to see the child regularly functioning in all seven intelligences. Consequently, comments like "loves finger painting," "moves gracefully during music and dance time," or "creates beautiful structures with blocks" can provide clues to a student's spatial, musical, or bodily-kinesthetic proclivities.

When reviewing a student's cumulative records, I've found it useful to photocopy the records (with permission from the school and parents, of course) and then take a yellow highlighting pen and underline all the positive information about that student, including the highest grades and test scores and the positive observations of others. Then I type up each piece of highlighted information on a separate sheet of paper and organize the sheets according to intelligences. This practice provides me with solid information about a student's strongest intelligences that I can then communicate to parents, administrators, and the student's teachers.

Talk with Other Teachers. If you have students only for English or math class, then you are usually not in a position to observe them displaying kinesthetic or musical gifts (unless, of course, you are regularly teaching through the multiple intelligences). Even if you work with students through all subject areas, you can often get additional information by contacting specialists who are working more specifically with one or two of the intelligences. Hence, the art teacher might be the best person to talk with about a student's spatial intelligence, the PE teacher the person to go to for information about some bodily-kinesthetic abilities, and the counselor the person who could share information about the personal intelligences (although the counselor's ability to share information may be limited due to issues of confidentiality). Regard your colleagues as important sources of assessment information about students' multiple intelligences and meet with them periodically to compare notes. You may find that a child who appears quite low functioning in one class will be one of the stars in a class that requires a different set of intelligences.

Talk with Parents. Parents are true experts of a child's multiple intelligences. They've had the opportunity to see the child learn and grow under a broad spectrum of circumstances encompassing all seven intelligences. Consequently, they ought to be enlisted in the effort to identify the child's strongest intelligences. During back-to-school night, parents should be introduced to the concept of multiple intelligences and be provided with specific ways through which they can observe and document their child's strengths at home, including the use of scrapbooks, audio cassettes, videotapes, photographs, and samples of stories, sketches, and artifacts that developed from a child's special hobby or other interest. Then, parents can bring to future parent-teacher conferences any information that may help teachers develop a broader understanding of the child's learning style.

Many years ago, the phrase "the six-hour retarded child" was used to describe a student who showed little promise or potential in the classroom but was a real achiever outside of school, perhaps as the leader of a youth group, a jack-of-all-trades that neighbors came to for all kinds of repairs, or a fledgling entrepreneur with a flourishing small business. Obtaining assessment information from the home is critical in discovering ways to transplant such a child's success from the home to the school.

Ask Students. Students are the ultimate experts on their learning style, because they've lived with it twenty-four hours a day ever since they were born. After they have been introduced to the idea of multiple intelligences (see Chapter 4), you can sit down with them and through an interview discover what *they* consider to be their strongest intelligences. I've used the "MI Pizza" shown in Figure 4.1 on page 39 as a record-keeping form for making notes while I ask students individually about their abilities in each area. You can also have students draw pictures of themselves doing things in their most developed intelligences (a spatial approach), rank from 1 to 7 their most developed to least developed intelligence on the MI Pizza (a logical-mathematical approach), or pantomime their most developed intelligences (a bodily-kinesthetic approach). Some of the activities in Chapter 4 can also be helpful in getting assessment data about students' multiple intelligences.

Set Up Special Activities. If you regularly teach through the multiple intelligences, then you have frequent opportunities to assess through the multiple intelligences as well. So, for example, if you teach a lesson on fractions seven different ways, you can note how different children respond to each activity. The child who is almost falling asleep during the logical presentation may come alive when the bodily-kinesthetic approach begins, only to tune out again when a musical method is used. Seeing little light bulbs go on and off during the course of a day is both an affirmation of the existence of these intelligences as well as a record of the individual differences in your class. Similarly, setting up activity centers for each intelligence (see Chapter 7) provides opportunities for seeing how students function in each area or which areas students naturally gravitate toward when they are free to choose. Since the MI perspective on assessment (presented in Chapter 10) is based on a close connection between instruction and assessment, many of the activities in Chapters 5 and 6 can be used as diagnostic indicators as well as teaching activities.

For Further Study

1. Fill out the inventory in Figure 3.1 for each student in your classroom. Notice which items cannot be answered for lack of sufficient background information about the student. Identify methods you can use to obtain information about these items (e.g., parent or child interview, experiential activities), and then use them to help complete the inventory. How does your view of individual children remain the same or change as a result of framing their lives in terms of MI theory? What implications do the inventory results have for your teaching?

2. Keep a journal to record observations of students' multiple intelligences. If you observe students outside the classroom (e.g., as a recess or lunchroom monitor) notice how their behavior is the same as or different from their behavior in the classroom. What evidence for each student's multiple intelligences emerges from the anecdotal data?

3. Select one form of documenting students' learning activities that you haven't yet tried, such as audiotaping, videotaping, or photography. Experiment with its use and notice how effective it may be in providing and communicating information about students' multiple intelligences.

4. Have students "tell" you their preferred intelligences through one or more of the following media: writing, drawing, pantomime, group discussion, personal interview. Make sure they have first been introduced to the theory through some of the activities described in Chapter 4.

5. During parent-teacher conferences, devote some time to acquiring information about a student's multiple intelligences at home.

6. Review selected students' cumulative files, focusing on data that suggest the presence of special proclivities in one or more of the seven intelligences. If possible, obtain copies of the file material so you can underline strengths with a yellow highlighter pen and then transcribe the highlighted items onto separate sheets of paper. Distribute these "strength profiles" at the next meeting called to discuss students' learning.

7. Conference with other teachers about students' multiple intelligences. Set aside special time so that teachers who are responsible for different intelligences in school (e.g., math, shop, art, literature, and music teachers) can reflect upon students' performance in each learning context.

4 Teaching Students About MI Theory

Give me a fish and I eat for a day.
Teach me to fish and I eat for a lifetime.

—Proverb

ONE OF THE MOST USEFUL FEATURES of MI theory is that it can be explained to a group of children as young as 1st grade in as little as five minutes in such a way that they can then use the MI vocabulary to talk about how they learn. While many other learning-style theories contain terms and acronyms not easily understood by adults, let alone children, the seven intelligences are yoked to concrete antecedents that young and old alike have had experience with: words, numbers, pictures, the body, music, people, and self.

Recent research in cognitive psychology applied to education has supported the notion that children benefit from instructional approaches that help them reflect upon their own learning processes (see Marzano 1988). When children engage in this kind of metacognitive activity, they can select appropriate strategies for problem solving. They can also serve as advocates for themselves when placed in new learning environments.

A Five-Minute Introduction to MI Theory

How does a teacher present the theory of multiple intelligences to a group of students? Naturally, the answer to that question will depend in part on the size of the class, the developmental level of students, their background, and the kinds of instructional resources available. The most direct way to introduce MI theory to students is simply to explain it to them. When I go to a new classroom to demonstrate how to teach a multiple-intelligence lesson, I always begin with a five-minute explanation of the theory so students have a context for understanding what I am doing there. I usually begin by asking, "How many of you think you're intelligent?" I've discovered that there seems to be an inverse relationship between the number of hands that go up and the grade level that I'm teaching—that is, the lower the grade level, the more hands go up; the higher the grade level, the fewer hands. This reminds me of NYU professor Neil Postman's remark that "children go into school as question marks and leave school as periods." What do we do in the intervening years to convince children that they're not intelligent?

Regardless of the number of hands that go up, I usually say, "All of you are intelligent—and not just in one way. Each of you is intelligent in seven different ways." I draw an "MI Pizza" on the blackboard (a circle divided into seven slices) and then begin to explain the model. "First, there is something called word smart." I use simple terms to describe the intelligences, since words like "linguistic" are a mouthful for many children. As shown in Figure 4.1, I also accompany each term with a graphic symbol to spatially reinforce it. Then I ask questions. "How many people here can speak?" Usually, I'll get a lot of hands with this question! "Well, in order to speak you have to use words, so all of you are word smart!" "How many people here can write?" "You're using words here also, so again, you're all word smart." Essentially, I ask questions that build *inclusion*. I steer clear of questions that might exclude lots of students, such as "How many of you have read fifteen books in the past month?" This is a learning model not for deciding which exclusive group one is a member of, but for celebrating *all* of one's potentials for learning. Otherwise, teachers might be preparing the way for students to say, "I don't have to read this book, because I'm really not word smart."

Here are the simple terms for each of the intelligences and some questions that I use in my presentations:

Linguistic Intelligence: Word Smart (see questions above)

Logical-Mathematical Intelligence: Number Smart or Logic Smart

- "How many of you can do math?"
- "How many people here have done a science experiment?"

Spatial Intelligence: Picture Smart

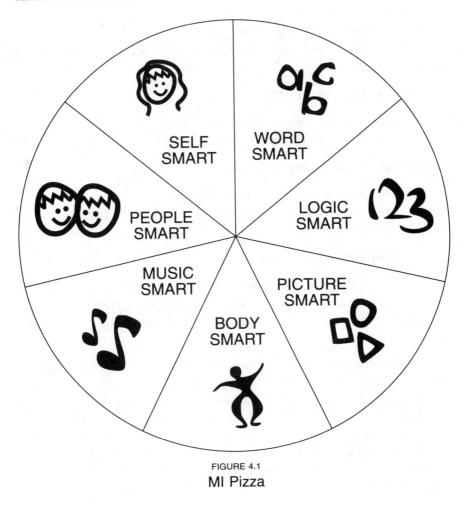

FIGURE 4.1
MI Pizza

• "How many of you draw?"
• "How many people here can see pictures in their head when they close their eyes?"
• "How many of you enjoy watching moving pictures on television, in the movies, or in a Nintendo game?"

Bodily-Kinesthetic Intelligence: Body Smart, Sports Smart, or Hand Smart (I use several terms here to get at different aspects of this intelligence.)

- "How many people here like sports?"
- "How many of you enjoy making things with your hands, like models or LEGO structures?"

Musical Intelligence: Music Smart

- "How many here enjoy listening to music?"
- "How many have ever played a musical instrument or sung a song?"

Interpersonal Intelligence: People Smart

- "How many people have at least one friend?"
- "How many of you enjoy working in groups at least part of the time here in school?"

Intrapersonal Intelligence: Self Smart

- "How many of you have a secret or special place you go to when you want to get away from everybody and everything?"
- "How many of you like to spend at least part of the time working on your own here in class?"

You can develop your own questions to illustrate each intelligence. Just make sure they build in *inclusion* and give all children a chance to see themselves as intelligent. You can also give examples of what Howard Gardner calls the "end-states" of each intelligence—that is, people who have developed an intelligence to a high level of competence. These examples provide students with models to be inspired by and to aspire to. Pick famous figures and heroes from each student's own world. Examples might include:

- *Word Smart:* authors of children's literature that the class has been reading

- *Number Smart or Logic Smart:* famous scientists students have studied in class

- *Picture Smart:* illustrators of children's literature, famous cartoonists and filmmakers

- *Body Smart:* famous sports heroes and actors

- *Music Smart:* famous rock stars, rappers, and other musicians

- *People Smart:* TV talk show hosts, politicians
- *Self Smart:* famous entrepreneurs ("self-made" people)

Activities for Teaching MI Theory

Naturally, you'll want to go beyond a simple verbal explanation of the model, and you should strive to teach the model in all seven intelligences. There are a number of ways of introducing the model or of following up your five-minute introduction with reinforcing activities and supplementary experiences. Here are some examples:

Career Day. If you regularly bring members of your community into the classroom to talk about their jobs, begin to contextualize this activity within a multiple-intelligence framework. Bring in an editor to talk about the kinds of "word smart" activities he uses, a tax accountant to speak about how she uses her "number smart" to help people, and an architect to explain the usefulness of "picture smart" in her career. Other career-day guests might include an athlete (body smart), a professional musician (music smart), a counselor (people smart), and a person who has started a business (self smart). Keep in mind, though, that each career usually involves several intelligences, and that you might want to discuss how each role brings together a combination of intelligences in a unique way. These presentations are extremely important in emphasizing to students that each of the intelligences plays a vital part in people's success in the world. You may want to speak beforehand with the guests about the model so they can work it into their presentations. Or you can simply follow up their appearances by relating what they said or did to one or more of the seven intelligences.

Field Trips. Take students to places in the community where each of the intelligences is particularly valued and practiced. Some destinations might include a library (word smart), a science lab (logic smart), a crafts factory (hand smart), a radio station that plays music (music smart), a public relations firm (people smart), and a psychologist's office (self smart). Again, seeing these intelligences in context gives students a more accurate "real-life" picture of MI theory than could ever be given in a classroom setting.

Biographies. Have students study the lives of well-known people proficient in one or more of the intelligences (see Gardner 1993b). Subjects for study might include Toni Morrison (word smart), Marie Curie (logic smart), Vincent Van Gogh (picture smart), Roberto Clemente (body smart), George Gershwin (music smart), Martin Luther King, Jr., (people smart), and Sigmund Freud (self smart). Make sure the people studied are representative of your students' cultural, racial, and ethnic backgrounds. See page 163 in Chapter 13 for more multicultural examples of famous people and page 137 in Chapter 11 for examples of famous people in each intelligence who overcame specific disabilities.

Lesson Plans. Teach a seven-way lesson on a particular subject or in a specific skill area (see Chapter 5 for guidelines on creating MI lessons). Explain beforehand to students that you are going to teach this material using each of the seven intelligences and that they should pay particular attention to *how* each of seven intelligences is covered. After the lesson, ask students to describe your use of each intelligence. This activity requires students to reflect upon the kinds of processes necessary for each intelligence and reinforces their metacognitive awareness. You may also want to ask them which particular method or methods they preferred. In this way, you help students begin to understand which strategies they prefer to use when learning something new.

Quick Experiential Activities. An experiential way of introducing MI theory is to have students complete seven activities, each of which draws primarily upon the use of one intelligence. For instance, you might have students do some writing ("write a short poem that you know"), math ("tell me how long ago was a million seconds ago"), drawing ("draw a picture of an animal"), running ("go outside and run to the end of the block and back"), singing ("let's all sing 'Row, Row, Row Your Boat' together"), sharing ("turn to a partner and share something nice that happened to you this week"), and self-reflecting ("close your eyes and think about the happiest moment in your life—you won't have to share it with anybody"). Adjust the activities to the ability level of your students, choosing activities that just about everyone can do, and giving those who can't do them modified versions of the activities. You can use this approach either before or after explicitly describing the "seven kinds of smart." Make sure to ask students which activities they prefer, and remember to relate each activity to one (or more) of the seven intelligences.

Wall Displays. Walk into a typical American classroom and you'll often find a poster of Albert Einstein on the wall. Einstein is probably a good representative of multiple intelligences because he used several of them in his work, including spatial, bodily-kinesthetic, and logical-mathematical. Instead of displaying an Einstein poster, however, consider hanging seven posters on the wall, each representing a person especially proficient in one of the intelligences (see Gardner 1993b and the "Biographies" section on pages 41–42 for suggested names). Or hang a banner reading "Seven Ways to Learn" or "This Is How We Learn in School" and display photos of students in the school using each of the intelligences. There are even commercially made posters on the seven intelligences, including one titled "Have You Used Your Seven Intelligences Today?" available from the Illinois Renewal Institute, 200 E. Wood Street, Suite 274, Palatine, IL 60067 (1-800-348-4474), and a seven-poster set (one for each intelligence) available from Zephyr Press, 3316 N. Chapel Ave., P.O. Box 66006-A, Tucson, AZ 85728-6006.

Shelf Displays. Show products made by students in the school that required the use of each of the seven intelligences. Examples might include essays, stories, or poems (word smart), computer programs (logic smart), drawings and paintings (picture smart), musical scores (music smart), three-dimensional projects (body smart), cooperative projects (people smart), and individual projects (self smart). The products could be displayed on a shelf, in a glass case, or on a table, and rotated regularly so all students have a chance to display their achievements. Make sure each product is labeled with the intelligence or intelligences required to produce it.

Readings. For older students, you can assign readings from any of the growing number of books and articles on the theory of multiple intelligences, including chapters from *Frames of Mind, 7 Kinds of Smart, In Their Own Way,* and *Seven Ways of Knowing.* Appendix B includes many more suggested readings.

MI Tables. Set up seven tables in the classroom, each clearly labeled with a sign referring to one of the seven intelligences. On each table, place a task card indicating what students are to do. At the word smart table, students can do a writing task; at the number smart table, a math or science task; at the picture smart table, a drawing task; at the body smart table, a building task; at the music smart table, a musical task; at the people smart table, a cooperative task; and at the self smart table, an individualized task. Tell students to go to the table they believe represents their most developed intelligence (don't tell them the tasks beforehand, or they will pick the table based on the activity). Have them work at the task for a designated amount of time (perhaps five minutes), and then use a musical signal (like a bell) to indicate that it's time to move to the next table (move clockwise). Continue until all students have experienced each task. Talk about students' preferences and relate each task to an intelligence. Chapter 7 deals more specifically with how to set up activity centers that reflect a multiple-intelligence perspective.

Human Intelligence Hunt. If you are introducing MI theory at the beginning of the year, when students still don't know each other very well, a "human intelligence hunt" is a useful way to teach students experientially about the seven kinds of smarts while helping them get to know one another better. It is based on the premise that each of us is a "treasure chest" filled with special gifts. These gifts are our intelligences. Sometimes, though, we're unaware of other people's gifts, so we have to go on a "treasure hunt"—in this case, an "intelligence hunt"—to discover one another's special talents. Each student receives a list of tasks like those in Figure 4.2. On your signal, students take the task sheet along

---

FIGURE 4.2
Human Intelligence Hunt

Find someone who can:

_____ whistle a few notes from Beethoven's Fifth Symphony.

_____ stand on one foot with her eyes closed for at least five seconds.

_____ recite at least four lines from any poem he has learned.

_____ draw a quick diagram explaining how an electric motor works.

_____ briefly share a dream she has had in the past two weeks.

_____ complete this numerical sequence: 36, 30, 24, 18, _____, and explain the logic behind it.

_____ honestly say he is relaxed and comfortable relating to other people during this exercise.

---

with a pen or pencil and find other students in the room who can do the tasks listed. There are three basic rules:

1. Students must actually *perform* the tasks listed, not simply say they can do them.

2. Once a student performs a task to the "hunter's" satisfaction, he or she should initial the blank space next to the appropriate task on the "hunter's" task sheet.

3. "Hunters" can ask a person to perform only one task; therefore, to complete the hunt, a student must have seven different sets of initials.

You can modify the activities listed in Figure 4.2 to include tasks geared to your students' aptitudes and abilities. For instance, if you're working with very young students, you may want to substitute the song "Old MacDonald Had a Farm" for Beethoven's Fifth Symphony. You can even create a hunt based entirely on pictures, which would involve students finding people in the class who particularly enjoy doing the kinds of activities depicted in each picture. After the activity, remember to link each task to a different intelligence and to talk about what students learned about one another's gifts or intelligences.

Board Games. You can create a homemade board game based on the seven intelligences. Get a manila file folder and a magic marker and create the common board game format of a winding roadway divided into many small squares. Assign each intelligence a color and then place an appropriately colored intelligence symbol on each square of the game board. You may use the symbols in Figure 4.1 or make up your own. Then create seven sets of 2" x 3" game cards from seven colors of paper that match the colored symbols on the game board. On each set of game cards, type or write tasks that involve using a specific intelligence. Here, for instance, are some tasks for picture smart at the primary level:

- Draw a picture of a dog in less than thirty seconds.
- Find an object in the shape of a circle in the class.
- Tell us your favorite color.
- Describe four blue things you see in the room.
- Close you eyes and describe the pictures in your mind.

Make sure most of the tasks are within the capabilities of your students. Then get a pair of dice and some miniature plastic figurines as game pieces, and start playing!

MI Stories, Songs, or Plays. Be creative and make up your own story, song, or play for teaching the idea of multiple intelligences (your students can help you). You might, for example, create a story about seven children, each an expert in a particular intelligence, who don't get along very well and who are forced into an adventure that requires them to travel to distant magical lands. In each land they encounter challenges that require the unique intelligence of a particular child. For example, the children come to a land where, in order to be understood, people have to communicate through singing, so the musical child guides them through this land. In another land, they fall into a hole and get out through the body-smart child's expertise. At the end of the story, they are able to accomplish their task (perhaps to retrieve a golden jewel) because they have drawn upon the talents or intelligences of all seven children.

This story can then be used as a metaphor for classroom behavior: we need to respect and find ways of celebrating the unique talents and gifts of each student. A story like this one could be performed as a play, a puppet show, or a musical and performed for other students in the school.

There are undoubtedly many other activities that would help teach students about the theory of multiple intelligences. The development of such experiences should be an ongoing process throughout the year. After you have introduced a few activities, it may be helpful to prominently display a poster listing the seven intelligences, perhaps in the form of the MI Pizza shown in Figure 4.1. When something happens that seems to relate to one or more of the seven intelligences, you can then use the poster to help emphasize the relationship. For example, if several students express a strong desire to work together on a project, you can point out that they want to use their "people smart." For a student who has created a particularly apt visual illustration for an assignment, you can suggest that she really employed her "picture smart" in the work. By modeling the practical use of MI theory frequently in the daily activities of the classroom, you will help students internalize the theory and you should begin to see them use its vocabulary to make sense out of their own learning lives.

For Further Study

1. Drawing upon the material in this chapter or activities of your own choosing, develop a way to introduce the theory of multiple intelligences to your students. Note their initial reactions. Follow this up with supplementary activities. How long does it take before students begin to use the terms themselves? Note two or three examples of how students used the model to explain their learning processes.

2. Create a mini-unit or special course for students on "learning about learning" that includes instruction in the theory of multiple intelligences. Include readings, exercises, activities, and strategies designed to help students understand their thinking styles so that they can learn more effectively.

3. Design a special wall display, bulletin board, or exhibit area where the seven intelligences are honored and celebrated. Include posters of famous people, photos of students engaged in MI activities, examples of products made by students in each of the intelligences, or all of these things.

5 MI and Curriculum Development

We do not see in our descriptions [of classroom activity] . . . much opportunity for students to become engaged with knowledge so as to employ their full range of intellectual abilities. And one wonders about the meaningfulness of whatever is acquired by students who sit listening or performing relatively repetitive exercises, year after year. Part of the brain, known as Magoun's brain, is stimulated by novelty. It appears to me that students spending twelve years in the schools we studied would be unlikely to experience much novelty. Does part of the brain just sleep, then?

—John I. Goodlad (1984, p. 231)

MI THEORY MAKES ITS GREATEST CONTRIBUTION to education by suggesting that teachers need to expand their repertoire of techniques, tools, and strategies beyond the typical linguistic and logical ones predominantly used in American classrooms. According to John Goodlad's pioneering "A Study of Schooling" project, which involved researchers in observing over 1,000 classrooms nationwide, nearly 70 percent of classroom time was consumed by "teacher" talk—mainly teachers talking "at" students (giving instructions, lecturing). The next most widely observed activity was students doing written assignments, and according to Goodlad (1984, p. 230), "much of this work was in the form of responding to directives in workbooks or on worksheets." In this context, the theory of multiple intelligences functions not only as a specific remedy to one-sidedness in teaching, but also as a "metamodel" for organizing and synthesizing all the educational innovations that have sought to break out of this narrowly confined approach to learning. In doing so, it provides a broad range of stimulating curricula to "awaken" the slumbering brains that Goodlad fears populate our nation's schools.

The Historical Background of Multimodal Teaching

Multiple intelligences as a philosophy guiding instruction is hardly a new concept. Even Plato, in a manner of speaking, seemed aware of the importance of multimodal teaching when he wrote: ". . . do not use compulsion, but let early education be a sort of amusement; you will then be better able to find out the natural bent" (Plato 1952, p. 399). More recently, virtually all the pioneers of modern education developed systems of teaching based upon more than verbal pedagogy. The 18th century philosopher Jean Jacques Rousseau declared in his classic treatise on education, *Emile,* that the child must learn not through words, but through experience; not through books but through "the book of life." The Swiss reformer Johann Heinrich Pestalozzi emphasized an integrated curriculum that regarded physical, moral, and intellectual training based solidly on concrete experiences. And the founder of the modern-day kindergarten, Friedrich Froebel, developed a curriculum consisting of hands-on experiences with manipulatives ("gifts"), playing games, singing songs, gardening, and caring for animals. In the 20th century, innovators like Maria Montessori and John Dewey evolved systems of instruction based upon multiple-intelligence-like techniques, including Montessori's tactile letters and other self-paced materials, and Dewey's vision of the classroom as a microcosm of society.

By the same token, many current alternative educational models essentially are multiple-intelligence systems using different terminologies (and with varying levels of emphasis upon the different intelligences). Cooperative learning, for example, seems to place its greatest emphasis upon interpersonal intelligence, yet specific activities can involve students in each of the other intelligences as well. Similarly, whole language instruction has at its core the cultivation of linguistic intelligence, yet it uses music, hands-on activities, introspection (through journal keeping), and group work to carry out its fundamental goals. Suggestopedia, a pedagogical approach developed by the Bulgarian psychiatrist Georgi Lozanov, uses drama and visual aids as keys to unlocking a student's learning potential, yet it seems that in this approach music plays the greatest role in facilitating learning, for students listen to music as an integral part of their instruction.

MI theory essentially encompasses what good teachers have always done in their teaching: reaching beyond the text and the blackboard to awaken students' minds.' Two recent movies about great teachers, *Stand and Deliver* (1987) and *Dead Poets Society* (1989), underline this point. In *Stand and Deliver,* Jaime Escalante (played by Edward James Olmos), a Hispanic high school mathematics teacher, uses apples to introduce fractions, fingers to teach multiplication, and imagery and metaphor to clarify negative numbers (if one digs a hole in the ground, the hole represents negative numbers, the pile of dirt next to it signifies positive numbers). John Keating (played by Robin Williams), the prep school instructor in *Dead Poets Society,* has students reading literary passages while kicking soccer balls and listening to classical music. MI theory provides a way for *all* teachers to reflect upon their best teaching methods and to understand why these methods work (or why they work well for some students but not for others). It also helps teachers expand their current teaching repertoire to include a broader range of methods, materials, and techniques for reaching an ever wider and more diverse range of learners.

The MI Teacher

A teacher in an MI classroom contrasts sharply with a teacher in a traditional classroom. In the traditional classroom, the teacher lectures while standing at the front of the classroom, writes on the blackboard, asks students questions about the assigned reading or handouts, and waits while students finish their written work. In the MI classroom, the teacher continually shifts her method of presentation from linguistic to spatial to musical and so on, often combining intelligences in creative ways.

The MI teacher may spend part of the time lecturing and writing on the blackboard at the front of the room. This, after all, is a legitimate teaching technique. Teachers have simply been doing too much of it. The MI teacher, however, also draws pictures on the blackboard or shows a videotape to illustrate an idea. She often plays music at some time during the day, either to set the stage for an objective, to make a point, or to provide an environment for study. The MI teacher provides hands-on experiences, whether this involves getting students up and moving about, or passing an artifact around to bring to life the material studied, or having students build something tangible to reveal their understanding. The MI teacher also has students interacting with each other in different ways (e.g., in pairs, small groups, or large groups), and she plans time for students to engage in self-reflection, undertake self-paced work, or link their personal experiences and feelings to the material being studied.

Such characterizations of what the MI teacher does and does not do, however, should not serve to rigidify the instructional dimensions of MI theory. The theory can be implemented in a wide range of instructional contexts, from highly traditional settings where teachers spend much of their time directly teaching students to open environments where students regulate most of their own learning. Even traditional teaching can take place in a variety of ways designed to stimulate the seven intelligences. The teacher who lectures with rhythmic emphasis (musical), draws pictures on the board to illustrate points (spatial), makes dramatic gestures as she talks (bodily-kinesthetic), pauses to give students time to reflect (intrapersonal), and asks questions that invite spirited interaction (interpersonal) is using MI principles within a teacher-centered perspective.

Key Materials and Methods of MI Teaching

There are a number of teaching tools in MI theory that go far beyond the traditional teacher-as-lecturer mode of instruction. Figure 5.1 provides a quick summary of MI teaching methods. The following list provides a broader, but still incomplete, survey of the techniques and materials that can be employed in teaching through the multiple intelligences. Capitalized items in the list are discussed more fully in Chapter 6.

Linguistic Intelligence

- lectures
- large- and small-group discussions
- books
- worksheets
- manuals
- BRAINSTORMING
- writing activities
- word games
- sharing time
- student speeches
- STORYTELLING
- talking books and cassettes
- extemporaneous speaking

52

FIGURE 5.1
Summary of the "Seven Ways of Teaching"

Intelligence	Teaching Activities (examples)	Teaching Materials (examples)	Instructional Strategies
Linguistic	lectures, discussions, word games, storytelling, choral reading, journal writing, etc.	books, tape recorders, typewriters, stamp sets, books on tape, etc.	read about it, write about it, talk about it, listen to it
Logical-Mathematical	brain teasers, problem solving, science experiments, mental calculation, number games, critical thinking, etc.	calculators, math manipulatives, science equipment, math games, etc.	quantify it, think critically about it, conceptualize it
Spatial	visual presentations, art activities, imagination games, mind-mapping, metaphor, visualization, etc.	graphs, maps, video, LEGO sets, art materials, optical illusions, cameras, picture library, etc.	see it, draw it, visualize it, color it, mind-map it,
Bodily-Kinesthetic	hands-on learning, drama, dance, sports that teach, tactile activities, relaxation exercises, etc.	building tools, clay, sports equipment, manipulatives, tactile learning resources, etc.	build it, act it out, touch it, get a "gut feeling" of it, dance it
Musical	superlearning, rapping, songs that teach	tape recorder, tape collection, musical instruments	sing it, rap it, listen to it
Interpersonal	cooperative learning, peer tutoring, community involvement, social gatherings, simulations, etc.	board games, party supplies, props for role plays, etc.	teach it, collaborate on it, interact with respect to it
Intrapersonal	individualized instruction, independent study, options in course of study, self-esteem building, etc.	self-checking materials, journals, materials for projects, etc.	connect it to your personal life, make choices with regard to it

Intelligence	Sample Educational Movement (primary intelligence)	Sample Teacher Presentation Skill	Sample Activity to Begin a Lesson
Linguistic	Whole Language	teaching through storytelling	long word on the blackboard
Logical-Mathematical	Critical Thinking	Socratic questioning	posing a logical paradox
Spatial	Integrated Arts Instruction	drawing/mind-mapping concepts	unusual picture on the overhead
Bodily-Kinesthetic	Hands-On Learning	using gestures/dramatic expressions	mysterious artifact passed around the class
Musical	Suggestopedia	using voice rhythmically	piece of music played as students come into class into class
Interpersonal	Cooperative Learning	dynamically interacting with students	"Turn to a neighbor and share . . ."
Intrapersonal	Individualized Instruction	bringing *feeling* into presentation	"Close your eyes and think of a time in your life when . . ."

- debates
- JOURNAL KEEPING
- choral reading
- individualized reading
- reading to the class
- memorizing linguistic facts
- TAPE RECORDING ONE'S WORDS
- using word processors
- PUBLISHING (e.g., creating class newspapers)

Logical-Mathematical Intelligence

- mathematical problems on the board
- SOCRATIC QUESTIONING
- scientific demonstrations
- logical problem-solving exercises
- CLASSIFICATIONS AND CATEGORIZATIONS
- creating codes
- logic puzzles and games
- QUANTIFICATIONS AND CALCULATIONS
- computer programming languages
- SCIENCE THINKING
- logical-sequential presentation of subject matter
- Piagetian cognitive stretching exercises
- HEURISTICS

Spatial Intelligence

- charts, graphs, diagrams, and maps
- VISUALIZATION
- photography
- videos, slides, and movies
- visual puzzles and mazes
- 3-D construction kits
- art appreciation
- imaginative storytelling
- PICTURE METAPHORS
- creative daydreaming
- painting, collage, and other visual arts

- IDEA SKETCHING
- visual thinking exercises
- GRAPHIC SYMBOLS
- using mind-maps and other visual organizers
- computer graphics software
- visual pattern seeking
- optical illusions
- COLOR CUES
- telescopes, microscopes, and binoculars
- visual awareness activities
- draw-and-paint/computer-assisted-design software
- picture literacy experiences

Bodily-Kinesthetic Intelligence

- creative movement
- HANDS-ON THINKING
- field trips
- mime
- THE CLASSROOM THEATER
- competitive and cooperative games
- physical awareness exercises
- hands-on activities of all kinds
- crafts
- BODY MAPS
- use of kinesthetic imagery
- cooking, gardening, and other "messy" activities
- manipulatives
- virtual reality software
- KINESTHETIC CONCEPTS
- physical education activities
- using body language/hand signals to communicate
- tactile materials and experiences
- physical relaxation exercises
- BODY ANSWERS

Musical Intelligence

- MUSICAL CONCEPTS

- singing, humming, or whistling
- playing recorded music
- playing live music on piano, guitar, or other instruments
- group singing
- MOOD MUSIC
- music appreciation
- playing percussion instruments
- RHYTHMS, SONGS, RAPS, AND CHANTS
- using background music
- linking old tunes with concepts
- DISCOGRAPHIES
- creating new melodies for concepts
- listening to inner musical imagery
- music software
- SUPERMEMORY MUSIC

Interpersonal Intelligence

- COOPERATIVE GROUPS
- interpersonal interaction
- conflict mediation
- peer teaching
- BOARD GAMES
- cross-age tutoring
- group brainstorming sessions
- PEER SHARING
- community involvement
- apprenticeships
- SIMULATIONS
- academic clubs
- interactive software
- parties or social gatherings as context for learning
- PEOPLE SCULPTING

Intrapersonal Intelligence

- independent study
- FEELING-TONED MOMENTS
- self-paced instruction

- individualized projects and games
- private spaces for study
- ONE-MINUTE REFLECTION PERIODS
- interest centers
- PERSONAL CONNECTIONS
- options for homework
- CHOICE TIME
- self-teaching programmed instruction
- exposure to inspirational/motivational curricula
- self-esteem activities
- journal keeping
- GOAL-SETTING SESSIONS

How to Create MI Lesson Plans

On one level, MI theory applied to the curriculum might best be represented by a loose and diverse collection of teaching strategies such as those listed above. In this sense, MI theory represents a model of instruction that has no distinct rules other than the demands imposed by the cognitive components of the intelligences themselves. Teachers can pick and choose from the above activities, implementing the theory in a way suited to their own unique teaching style and congruent with their educational philosophy (as long as that philosophy does not declare that all children learn in the same way).

On a deeper level, however, MI theory suggests a set of parameters within which educators can create new curricula. In fact, the theory provides a context within which educators can address any skill, content area, theme, or instructional objective, and develop at least seven ways to teach it. Essentially, MI theory offers a means of building daily lesson plans, weekly units, or monthly or year-long themes and programs in such a way that all students can have their strongest intelligences addressed at least some of the time.

The best way to approach curriculum development using the theory of multiple intelligences is by thinking about how we *can translate* the material to be taught from one intelligence to another. In other words, how can we take a linguistic symbol system, such as the English language, and translate it—not into other linguistic languages, such as Spanish or French, but into the languages of other intelligences, namely, pictures, physical or musical expression, logical symbols or concepts, social interactions, and intrapersonal connections?

The following seven-step procedure suggests one way to create lesson plans or curriculum units using MI theory as an organizing framework:

1. Focus on a Specific Objective or Topic. You might want to develop curricula on a large scale (e.g., for a year-long theme) or create a program for reaching a specific instructional objective (e.g., for a student's individualized education plan). Whether you have chosen "ecology" or "the schwa sound" as a focus, however, make sure you have clearly and concisely stated the objective. Place the objective or topic in the center of a sheet of paper, as shown below in Figure 5.2.

2. Ask Key MI Questions. Figure 5.2 shows the kinds of questions to ask when developing a curriculum for a specific objective or topic. These questions can help prime the creative pump for the next steps.

FIGURE 5.2
MI Planning Questions

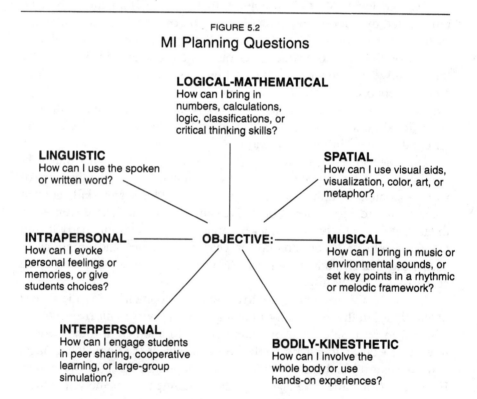

LOGICAL-MATHEMATICAL
How can I bring in numbers, calculations, logic, classifications, or critical thinking skills?

LINGUISTIC
How can I use the spoken or written word?

SPATIAL
How can I use visual aids, visualization, color, art, or metaphor?

INTRAPERSONAL
How can I evoke personal feelings or memories, or give students choices?

OBJECTIVE:

MUSICAL
How can I bring in music or environmental sounds, or set key points in a rhythmic or melodic framework?

INTERPERSONAL
How can I engage students in peer sharing, cooperative learning, or large-group simulation?

BODILY-KINESTHETIC
How can I involve the whole body or use hands-on experiences?

3. Consider the Possibilities. Look over the questions in Figure 5.2, the list of MI techniques and materials in Figure 5.1, and the descriptions of specific strategies in Chapter 6. Which of the methods and materials seem most appropriate? Think of other possibilities not listed that might be appropriate.

4. Brainstorm. Using an MI Planning Sheet like the one shown below in Figure 5.3, begin listing as many teaching approaches as possible for each intelligence. You should end up with something like the sheet shown in Figure 5.4 on the next page. When listing approaches, be specific about the topic you want to address (e.g., "videotape of rain forest" rather than simply "videotape"). The rule of thumb for brainstorming is "list *everything* that comes to mind." Aim for at least twenty or thirty ideas and at least one idea for each intelligence. Brainstorming with colleagues may help stimulate your thinking.

5. Select Appropriate Activities. From the ideas on your completed planning sheet, circle the approaches that seem most workable in your educational setting.

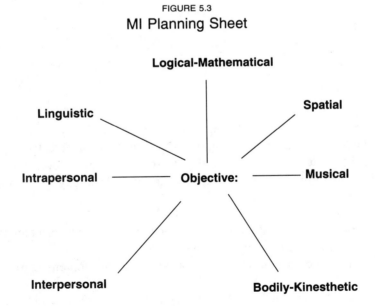

FIGURE 5.3
MI Planning Sheet

FIGURE 5.4
Completed MI Planning Sheet

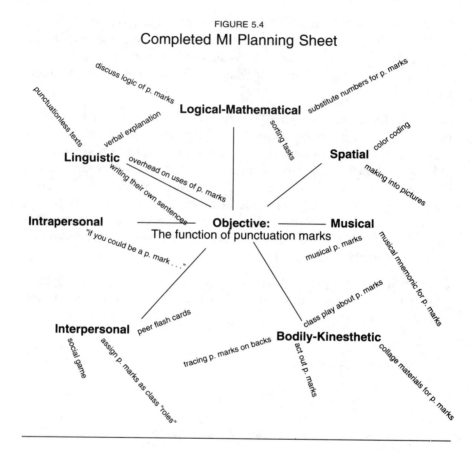

6. Set Up a Sequential Plan. Using the approaches you've selected, design a lesson plan or unit around the specific topic or objective chosen. Figure 5.5 shows what a seven-day lesson plan might look like when perhaps thirty-five to forty minutes of class time each day are allotted to the objective.

7. Implement the Plan. Gather the materials needed, select an appropriate time frame, and then carry out the lesson plan. Modify the lesson as needed to incorporate changes that occur during implementation.

Appendix C contains additional examples of MI lessons and programs.

FIGURE 5.5
Sample Seven-Day MI Lesson Plan

Level: 4th grade

Subject: Language arts

Objective: To understand the function of, and differences between, four punctuation marks: the question mark, period, comma, and exclamation mark.

Monday (Linguistic Intelligence): Students listen to a verbal explanation of the function of punctuation marks, read sentences having examples of each mark, and complete a worksheet requiring them to fill in their own marks.

Tuesday (Spatial Intelligence): The teacher draws on the board graphic images that correspond in meaning and form to each mark (Question mark = a hook, since questions "hook" us into requiring an answer; exclamation point = a staff that you pound on the floor when you want to exclaim something; a period = a point, since you've just made your point, plain and simple; and a comma = a brake pedal, since it requires you to temporarily stop in the middle of a sentence. Students can make up their own images and then place them as pictures in sentences (with different colors assigned to different marks).

Wednesday (Bodily-Kinesthetic Intelligence): The teacher asks students to use their bodies to form the shapes of the different punctuation marks as she reads sentences requiring these marks (e.g., a curved body posture for question mark).

Thursday (Musical Intelligence): Students make up different sounds for the punctuation marks (as Victor Borge did in his comedy routines), and then make these sounds in unison as different students read sample sentences requiring the use of the four marks.

Friday (Logical-Mathematical Intelligence): Students form groups of four to six. Each group has a box divided into four compartments, each of which is assigned a punctuation mark. The groups sort sentence stubs with missing punctuation marks (one per sentence stub) into the four compartments according to the punctuation needed.

Monday (Interpersonal Intelligence): Students form groups of four to six. Each student has four cards, and each card has a different punctuation mark written on it. The teacher places a sentence requiring a given punctuation mark on the overhead projector. As soon as students see the sentence, they toss the relevant card in the center of their group's circle. The first student in the group to throw in a correct card gets five points, the second four, and so on.

Tuesday (Intrapersonal Intelligence): Students are asked to create their own sentences using each of the punctuation marks; the sentences should relate to their personal lives (e.g., a question they'd like somebody to answer, a statement they feel strongly about, a fact they know that they'd like others to know about).

MI and Thematic Instruction

More and more educators are recognizing the importance of teaching students from an interdisciplinary point of view. Although academic skill teaching or the teaching of isolated chunks of knowledge may provide students with competencies or background information that can prove useful to them in their further education, such instruction often fails to connect students to the real world—a world that they will have to function in as citizens a few years hence. Consequently, educators are turning toward models of instruction that more closely imitate or mirror life in some significant way. Such instruction is frequently *thematic* in nature. Themes cut through traditional curricular boundaries, weave together subjects and skills that are found naturally in life, and provide students with opportunities to use their multiple intelligences in practical ways. As Susan Kovalik (1993, p. 5), developer of the Integrated Thematic Instruction (ITI) model, puts it:

> A key feature of *here and now* curriculum is that it is immediately recognized (by the student) as being relevant and meaningful.... Furthermore, it purports to teach our young about their world and the skills necessary to act within and upon it, thus preparing them- selves for living the fast-paced changes of the 1990's and beyond.

Kovalik's ITI model is based on year-long themes (such as "What Makes It Tick?") that are themselves made up of month-long components (such as clocks/time, electrical power, transportation) and weekly topics (such as seasonal change and geologic time). Other curricular approaches focus on alternative time frames, such as semester units or three-month themes. Regardless of the time element involved, MI theory provides a context for structuring thematic curricula. It provides a way of making sure the activities selected for a theme will activate all seven intelligences and therefore draw upon every child's inner gifts.

Figure 5.6 outlines the kinds of activities that might be used for the theme "Inventions." It shows how activities can be structured to address traditional academic subjects as well as each of the seven intelligences. Significantly, this chart illustrates how science activities needn't focus only on logical-mathematical intelligence and how language activities (reading and writing) needn't focus only on linguistic intelligence; they can, in fact, span all seven intelligences.

Keep in mind that MI theory can be applied to the curriculum in a variety of ways. There are no standard guidelines to follow. The ideas in

FIGURE 5.6

MI and Thematic Instruction

Sample Theme: Inventions

	Math	Science	Reading	Writing	Social Studies
Linguistic	Read math problems involving inventions	Talk about the basic scientific principles involved in specific inventions	Read a general book about inventions	Write about what you'd like to invent	Write about the social conditions that gave rise to certain inventions
Logical-Mathematical	Learn a math formula that served as the basis for an invention	Create a hypothesis for the development of a new invention	Read a book about the logic and math behind inventions	Write a word problem based on a famous invention	Create a time line of famous inventions
Spatial	Sketch the geometry involved in specific inventions	Draw a new or existing invention showing all working parts	Read a book with lots of diagrams of the inner workings of inventions	Label the individual components of your drawing of an invention	Paint a mural showing inventions in social/historical context
Bodily-Kinesthetic	Create an invention to measure a specific physical activity	Build your own invention based on sound scientific principles	Read the instructions for putting together an existing invention	Write instructions for building your own invention from scrap materials	Put on a play about how a certain invention came to be
Musical	Study the math involved in the invention of musical instruments	Study the science behind the invention of electronic music	Read about the background to invention songs such as "John Henry"	Write the lyrics for a song promoting a new invention	Listen to music about inventions at different historical periods
Interpersonal	Be in a study group that looks at the mathematics involved in specific inventions	Form a discussion group to study the science behind inventions	Read about the cooperation necessary for developing an invention	Write a play about inventions that can be put on by the class	Hold a discussion group about how a certain invention came to be
Intrapersonal	Create your own word problems based on inventions	Develop a self-study program to examine the scientific basis for a specific invention	Read the biography of a famous inventor	Write your personal autobiography as a "famous inventor"	Think about this question: if you could invent a time machine, where would you go?

this chapter are suggestions only; I invite you to create other forms or formulas for lesson planning or thematic development, and I encourage you to incorporate other formats, including those developed by educators such as Kovalik (1993) and Hunter (see Gentile 1988). Ultimately, you should be guided by your deepest and sincerest attempts to reach beyond the intelligences you may currently be teaching to, so that every child has the opportunity to succeed in school.

For Further Study

1. Look over the list of teaching strategies in this chapter. Circle the strategies you use or have used in your instruction. Place a yellow star next to the approaches that have worked best. Place a red flag next to the activities you think you use too much. Finally, place a blue arrow pointing upwards next to new activities you would like to try.

Over the next few weeks, eliminate or scale back your use of some of the red flagged/overused techniques, increase the time you spend using the yellow-starred approaches, and add to your teaching repertoire some of the blue-arrowed techniques.

2. Select a specific skill or instructional objective that many of your students don't seem to be effectively learning. Apply the seven-step planning process described in this chapter to generate a multiple-intelligence lesson or series of lessons, and then teach your students using the activities you've developed.

Afterward, reflect upon the lesson. Which parts were most successful? Which were least successful? Ask students to reflect upon the lesson in the same way. What have you learned from this experience that can help you regularly teach through multiple intelligences?

3. Select a theme to serve as a basis for a curriculum in your class. Use the seven-step lesson-planning process described in this chapter to generate a basic framework of activities that includes all seven intelligences and each academic subject area. (Refer to Figure 5.6 for guidance in developing activities.)

4. Focus on an intelligence that you usually don't touch upon in your teaching, create a lesson plan that includes it, and teach the lesson to your students. (See Appendix B for instructional resources in each intelligence.)

6 MI and Teaching Strategies

If the only tool you have is a hammer,
Everything around you looks like a nail.

—Anonymous

MI THEORY OPENS THE DOOR TO A WIDE variety of teaching strategies that can be easily implemented in the classroom. In many cases, they are strategies that have been used for decades by good teachers. In other cases, the theory of multiple intelligences offers teachers an opportunity to develop innovative teaching strategies that are relatively new to the educational scene. In either case, MI theory suggests that no one set of teaching strategies will work best for all students at all times. All children have different proclivities in the seven intelligences, so any particular strategy is likely to be highly successful with one group of students and less successful with other groups. For example, teachers who use Rhythms, Raps, and Chants (see below) as a pedagogical tool will probably find that musically inclined students respond enthusiastically to this strategy while nonmusical students remain unmoved. Similarly, the use of pictures and images in teaching will reach students who are more spatially oriented but perhaps have a different effect on those who are more physically or verbally inclined.

Because of these individual differences among students, teachers are best advised to use a broad range of teaching strategies with their students. As long as instructors shift their intelligence emphasis from presentation to presentation, there will always be a time during the period or day when a student has his or her own most highly developed intelligence(s) actively involved in learning.

In this chapter, I present thirty-five teaching strategies, five for each of the seven intelligences. The strategies are designed to be general enough so you can apply them at any grade level, yet specific enough so that little guesswork is required to implement them. Keep in mind that these are only a few samples of some of the better strategies available (see Chapter 5 for a list of more strategies). I encourage you to find additional strategies or to develop your own unique adaptations of existing strategies.

Teaching Strategies for Linguistic Intelligence

Linguistic intelligence is perhaps the easiest intelligence to develop strategies for, because so much attention has been given to its cultivation in the schools. I do not include the traditional linguistic strategies involving textbooks, worksheets, and lectures among the five strategies discussed here, however, simply because they have been overused. This is not to say that textbooks, worksheets, and lectures should never be used. They serve as excellent channels for effectively imparting certain kinds of information. But they are only *one small part* of a vast repertoire of teaching strategies—and not necessarily the most important part. Though used extensively in schools all over the United States, this trio of teaching techniques most easily reaches only a segment of the learning population: the most "book-oriented" and "lecture-gifted" students. The five strategies described below are accessible to a broader range of learners because they emphasize open-ended language activities that bring out the linguistic intelligence in *every* learner.

Storytelling. Storytelling has traditionally been seen as entertainment for children in the library or during special enrichment times in the classroom. Storytelling should be viewed as a vital teaching tool, for so it has been in cultures all over the world for thousands of years. When using storytelling in the classroom, you weave essential concepts, ideas, and instructional goals into a story that you tell directly to students. Although storytelling is usually thought of as a means of conveying knowledge in the humanities, it can be applied in mathematics and science as well. For example, to teach the idea of multiplication, you can tell students the story of a group of brothers and sisters who have magical powers: whatever they touch multiplies (for the first child, it doubles; for the second, it triples, and so on). To convey the notion of centrifugal force, you can take students on a mythical journey to a land where everything spins around very rapidly.

Prepare for storytelling by listing the essential elements you'd like to include in the story. Then use your imagination to create a special land, a group of colorful characters, and a whimsical plot to carry the message home. It may help to visualize the story at first, and then practice telling it to a spouse or to a mirror. Stories needn't be especially original or fabulous for children to benefit from them. Students are often impressed simply by a teacher's willingness to be creative and speak from the heart about a subject.

Brainstorming. Lev Vygotsky once said that a thought is like a cloud shedding a shower of words. During brainstorming, students produce a torrent of verbal thoughts that can be collected and put on the board or an overhead transparency. The brainstorming can be about anything: words for a class poem, ideas for developing a group project, thoughts about material in a lesson being taught, suggestions for a class picnic, and so forth. The general rules for brainstorming are: share whatever comes to mind that is relevant, no put-downs or criticisms of any idea, and *every* idea counts. You can place ideas at random on the board, or use a special system (such as an outline, a mind-map, or a Venn diagram) for organizing them. After everyone has had a chance to share, look for patterns or groupings in the ideas, invite students to reflect on the ideas, or use the ideas in a specific project (as in a group poem). This strategy allows all students who have an idea to be given special acknowledgement for their original thoughts.

Tape Recording. The tape recorder is probably one of the most valuable learning tools in any classroom. This is because it offers students a medium through which to learn about their linguistic powers and helps them employ verbal skills to communicate, solve problems, and express inner feelings. Students can use a tape recorder to "talk out loud" about a problem they are attempting to solve or a project they are planning to do. In this way, they reflect upon their own problem-solving processes or cognitive skills. They can also use the tape recorder to prepare for writing, helping to loosen the soil, so to speak, of their topic. Students who are not good writers may also want to record their thoughts on tape as an alternative mode of expression. Some students may use the tape recorder to send "oral letters" to other students in the class, to share personal experiences, and to get feedback about how they are coming across to others in the classroom.

The tape recorder can be used as a *collector* of information—in interviews, for example—and as a *reporter* of information—as in talking books. Tape recorders can also be used to provide information. For instance, one can be placed in each activity center so students can listen to information about the topic in that center. Every classroom should have several tape recorders available, and teachers should plan on using them regularly to promote the growth of students' minds.

Journal Writing. Keeping a personal journal involves students in making ongoing written records related to a specific domain. The domain can be broad and open-ended ("Write about anything you're thinking about or feeling during the class day") or quite specific ("Use this journal to keep a simulated record of your life as a farmer during the 1800s as part of our history course"). Journals can be kept in math ("Write about problem-solving strategies you use"), science ("Keep a record of the experiments you do, hypotheses you're testing, and new ideas that emerge from your work"), literature ("Keep an ongoing record of your responses to the books you're reading"), or other subjects. They can be kept entirely private, shared only between teacher and student, or regularly read to the class. They can also incorporate multiple intelligences by allowing drawings, sketches, photos, dialogues, and other nonverbal data. (Note that this strategy also draws heavily upon intrapersonal intelligence insofar as students work individually and use the journal to reflect upon their lives.)

Publishing. In traditional classrooms, students complete papers that are turned in, graded, and then often thrown away. Many students exposed to this kind of routine begin to see writing as the dreary process of fulfilling an assignment. Educators ought to be sending students a different message: that writing is a powerful tool for communicating ideas and influencing people. By providing students with opportunities to publish and distribute their work, you can make this point in a strong way.

Publishing takes many forms. Students might write on ditto masters and have many copies run off. Their writings can be photocopied and distributed or keyed into a word-processing program and printed in multiple copies. Students can submit their writing to a class or school newspaper, a city newspaper, a children's magazine, or some other publishing source that accepts student work. Students' writing can also be bound in book form and made available in a special section of the class or school library.

After publication, encourage interaction between the authors and the readers. You might even have special student autographing parties and book circles to discuss students' writings. When children see that others care enough about their writing to duplicate it, discuss it, and even argue about it, they become linguistically empowered and are motivated to continue developing their writing craft.

Teaching Strategies for Logical-Mathematical Intelligence

Typically, logical-mathematical thinking is restricted to math and science courses. There are components of this intelligence, however, that are applicable throughout the curriculum. The emergence of the critical-thinking movement certainly suggests one broad way in which logical-mathematical intelligence has affected the social sciences and humanities. Similarly, the call for "numeracy" (the logical-mathematical equivalent of "literacy") in our schools and, in particular, the recommendation that mathematics be applied to an interdisciplinary curriculum point to the wide application of this form of thinking to every part of the school day. The following are five major strategies for developing logical-mathematical intelligence that can be employed in all school subjects:

Calculations and Quantifications. In line with current reform efforts, teachers are being encouraged to discover opportunities to talk about numbers both inside and outside the math and science arena. In subjects such as history and geography, you may focus regularly on important statistics: lives lost in wars, populations of countries, and so forth. But how do you accomplish the same aim in literature? You shouldn't force connections that simply aren't there. It's surprising, however, how many novels, short stories, and other literary works make reference to numbers. In a novel by Virginia Woolf, there is a mention of fifty pounds to fix a greenhouse roof. How does that figure translate into U.S. dollars? In a short story by Doris Lessing, a boy must count to see how long he can stay underwater and then compare that to the amount of time it takes experienced divers to swim through a submerged tunnel. Each of these passages provides the basis for some mathematical thinking. Of course, you shouldn't feel compelled to make word problems out of great works of art—that would be stifling to say the least. It is a good idea, however, to keep alert for interesting numbers and intriguing math problems wherever they may be found. By tuning into the numbers in the midst of nonmathematical subjects, you can better engage highly logical students, and other students can learn to see that math belongs not just in math class but in life.

Classifications and Categorizations. The logical mind can be stimulated anytime information (whether it be linguistic, logical-mathematical, spatial, or other kinds of data) is put into some kind of rational framework. For example, in a unit on the effects of climate on culture, students might brainstorm a random list of geographic locations and then classify them by type of climate (e.g., desert, mountain, plains, or tropical). Or, in a science unit on states of matter, the instructor might put the names of three categories—Gas, Liquid, Solid—at the top of columns on the blackboard and then ask students to list examples of things belonging to each category. Other examples of logical-frameworks include: Venn diagrams, time lines, attribute webs (listing the attributes of a person, place, or thing as spokes around the subject), 5W organizers (diagrams that answer who, what, when, where, and why), and mind-maps. Most of these frameworks are also spatial in nature. The value of this approach is that disparate fragments of information can be organized around central ideas or themes, making them easier to remember, discuss, and think about.

Socratic Questioning. The critical-thinking movement has provided an important alternative to the traditional image of the teacher as knowledge dispenser. In Socratic questioning, the teacher serves as a questioner of students' points of view. The Greek sage Socrates is the model for this type of instruction. Instead of talking *at* students, the teacher participates in dialogues *with* them, aiming to uncover the rightness or wrongness of their beliefs. Students share their hypotheses about how the world works, and the teacher guides the "testing" of these hypotheses for clarity, precision, accuracy, logical coherence, or relevance through artful questioning. A history student who declares that World War II never would have happened if soldiers had actively resisted military service has his point of view subjected to rigorous scrutiny in this approach to teaching. A student defending the motives of a character in *Huckleberry Finn* is carefully questioned to see if her stand is supported by the facts in the novel. The purpose is not to humiliate students or put them in the wrong, but rather to help them sharpen their own critical thinking skills so that they no longer form opinions simply out of strong emotion or the passion of the moment (see Paul 1992).

Heuristics. The field of heuristics refers to a loose collection of strategies, rules of thumb, guide lines, and suggestions for logical problem solving. In terms of this book's goals, however, heuristics can be regarded as a major teaching/learning strategy. Examples of heuristic principles include: finding analogies to the problem you wish to solve, separating the various parts of the problem, proposing a possible solution to the problem and then working backwards, and finding a problem related to yours and then solving it. While the most obvious applications of heuristics are in the math and science fields, heuristic principles can also be used in subjects other than logical-mathematical ones. In trying to envision solutions to the problems of government waste, for example, a student might look for analogies by asking himself what other entities create waste. While looking for the main idea in a reading passage, a student might separate out each part of the passage (into sentences) and subject each part to qualifying "tests" of a key point. Heuristics provides students with logical maps, so to speak, to help them find their way around unfamiliar academic terrain (see Polya 1957).

Science Thinking. Just as you should look for mathematics in every part of the curriculum, so too should you seek out scientific ideas in areas other than science. This strategy is especially important given research showing that up to 95 percent of adults lack a fundamental knowledge of scientific vocabulary and demonstrate a poor understanding of the impact of science on the world ("Poll Finds Americans Are Ignorant of Science" 1988). There are ways to spread science thinking across the curriculum. For instance, students can study the influence important scientific ideas have had on history (e.g., how the development of the atomic bomb influenced the outcome of World War II). They can study science fiction with an eye toward discovering if the ideas described are feasible. They can learn about global issues—such as AIDs, overpopulation, and the greenhouse effect—that require some science background to be well understood. In each part of the curriculum, science provides another point of view that can considerably enrich students' perspective.

Teaching Strategies for Spatial Intelligence

The cave drawings of prehistoric man are evidence that spatial learning has long been important to human beings. Unfortunately, in today's schools the idea of presenting information to students through visual as well as auditory modes sometimes translates into simply writing on the board, a practice that is linguistic in nature. Spatial intelligence responds to *pictures*, either the images in one's mind or the images in the external world: photos, slides, movies, drawings, graphic symbols, ideographic languages, and so forth. Here are five teaching strategies designed to activate students' spatial intelligence:

Visualization. One of the easiest ways to help students translate book and lecture material into pictures and images is to have them close their eyes and picture whatever is being studied. One application of this strategy involves having students create their own "inner blackboard" (or movie or TV screen) in their mind's eye. They can then place on this mental blackboard any material they need to remember: spelling words, math formulas, history facts, or other data. When asked to recall a specific body of information, students then need only call up their mental blackboard and "see" the data inscribed on it.

A more open-ended application of this strategy involves having students close their eyes and see pictures of what they've just read or studied (e.g., a story or a chapter in a textbook). Afterward, they can draw or talk about their experiences. Teachers can also lead students through more formal "guided imagery" sessions as a way of introducing them to new concepts or material (e.g., leading them on a "guided tour" through the circulatory system to learn anatomy). Students may experience nonspatial content as well during these activities (e.g., kinesthetic images, verbal images, or musical images).

Color Cues. Highly spatial students are often sensitive to color. Unfortunately, the school day is usually filled with black-and-white texts, copy books, worksheets, and chalkboards. There are, however, many creative ways of putting color into the classroom as a learning tool. Use a variety of colors of chalk, markers, and transparencies when writing in front of the class. Provide students with colored pencils and pens, and colored paper on which to write assignments. Students can learn to use different colored markers to "color code" material they are studying (e.g., mark all the key points in red, all the supporting data in green, all the unclear passages in orange). Use color to emphasize patterns, rules, or classifications during instruction (e.g., coloring all *th*'s red in a phonics lesson; using different colors to write about distinct historical stages in Greek history). Finally, students can use their favorite colors as a stress reducer when coping with difficult problems (e.g., "If you run into a word, problem, or idea you don't understand, imagine your favorite color filling your head; this can help you find the right answer or clarify things for yourself").

Picture Metaphors. A metaphor is using one idea to refer to another, and a picture metaphor expresses an idea in a visual image. Developmental psychologists suggest that young children are masters of metaphor (see Gardner 1979). Sadly, this capacity often diminishes as children grow older. However, educators can tap this underground stream (to use a metaphor!) to help students master new material. The educational value of metaphor lies in establishing connections between what a student already knows and what is being presented. Think of the key point or main concept you want students to master. Then link that idea to a visual image. Construct the complete metaphor yourself (e.g., "How is the development of the colonies during early American history like the growth of an amoeba?") or have students develop their own (e.g., "If the major organs in the body were animals, which ones would they be?").

Idea Sketching. A review of some of the notebooks of eminent individuals in history, including Charles Darwin, Thomas Edison, and Henry Ford, reveals that these people used simple drawings in developing many of their powerful ideas. Teachers should recognize the value this kind of visual thinking can have in helping students articulate their understanding of subject matter. The Idea Sketching strategy involves asking students to draw the key point, main idea, central theme, or core concept being taught. Neatness and realism should be deemphasized in favor of a succession of quick sketches that help articulate an idea.

To prepare students for this kind of drawing, it may be helpful to play the game Pictionary or Win, Lose or Draw so students are used to the notion of making rapid drawings that convey central ideas. Then, begin to ask students to draw the concept or idea you want to focus on in a lesson. This strategy can be used to evaluate a student's understanding of an idea, to emphasize a concept, or to give students ample opportunity to explore an idea in greater depth. Here are some examples of subjects or concepts you might have students choose to illustrate: the Great Depression, gravity, probability (in math), fractions, democracy, pathos (in a literary work), ecosystem, and continental drift. Following up the drawing activity with a discussion of the relationship between the drawings and the subject matter is important. Do not evaluate the drawings themselves; instead, seek to "draw out" students' understanding from the sketches (see McKim 1980).

Graphic Symbols. One of the most traditional teaching strategies involves writing words on a blackboard. Less common, especially after primary school, is *drawing pictures* on the board, even though pictures may be extremely important to the understanding of the spatially inclined student. Consequently, teachers who can support their teaching with drawings and graphic symbols as well as words may be reaching a wider range of learners. This strategy, then, requires you to practice *drawing* at least some part of your lessons—for instance, by creating graphic symbols that depict the concepts to be learned. Here are some examples:

• Showing the three states of matter by drawing a solid mass (heavy chalk marks), a liquid mass (lighter curvy marks), and a gaseous mass (little dots).

• Indicating "root words" by putting little roots at the base of those words on the board.

• Drawing a time line for a novel's plot or historical event and marking the line not only with dates and names but also with pictures that symbolize events.

You do not need superior drawing skills to use this strategy; roughly drawn graphic symbols will suffice in most cases. Your willingness to model imperfect drawing can actually serve as an example for students who feel shy about sharing their own drawing with the class.

Teaching Strategies for Bodily-Kinesthetic Intelligence

Students may leave their textbooks and folders behind when they leave school, but they take their bodies with them wherever they go. Consequently, finding ways to help students integrate learning at a 'gut" level can be very important to increasing their retention and understanding. Traditionally, physical learning has been considered the province of P.E. and vocational education. The following strategies, however, show how easy it is to integrate hands-on and kinesthetic learning activities into traditional academic subjects like reading, math, and science.

Body Answers. Ask students to respond to instruction by using their bodies as a medium of expression. The simplest and most over-used example of this strategy is asking students to raise their hands to indicate understanding. This strategy can be varied in any number of ways, however. Instead of raising hands, students could smile, blink one eye, hold up fingers (one finger to indicate just a little understanding, five fingers to show complete understanding), make flying motions with their arms, and so forth. Students can provide "body answers" during a lecture ("If you understand what I've just said, put your finger on your temple; if you don't understand, scratch your head"), while going through a textbook ("Anytime you come to something in the text that seems outdated, I want you to frown"), or in answering questions that have a limited number of answers ("If you think this sentence has parallel construction, I want you to raise your two hands high like a referee indicating a touchdown; if you think it's not parallel, put your hands together over your head like the peak of a house").

The Classroom Theater. To bring out the actor in each of your students, ask them to enact the texts, problems, or other material to be learned by dramatizing or role playing the content. For example, students might dramatize a math problem involving three-step problem solving by putting on a three-act play. Classroom theater can be as informal as a one-minute improvisation of a reading passage during class or as formal as a one-hour play at the end of the semester that sums up students' understanding of a broad learning theme. It can be done without any materials or it may involve substantial use of props. Students may themselves act in plays and skits, or they may produce puppet shows or dramatizations in miniature (e.g., showing how a battle was fought by putting miniature soldiers on a plywood battlefield and moving them around to show troop movements). To help older students who may initially feel reluctant to engage in dramatic activities, try some warm-up exercises (see Spolin 1986).

Kinesthetic Concepts. The game of charades has long been a favorite of party-goers because of the way it challenges participants to express knowledge in unconventional ways. The Kinesthetic Concepts strategy involves either introducing students to concepts through physical illustrations or asking students to pantomime specific concepts or terms from the lesson. This activity requires students to translate information from linguistic or logical symbol systems into purely bodily-kinesthetic expression. The range of subjects is endless. Here are just a few examples of concepts that might be expressed through physical gestures or movements: soil erosion, cell mitosis, political revolution, supply and demand, subtraction (of numbers), the epiphany (of a novel), and biodiversity in an ecosystem. Simple pantomimes can also be extended into more elaborate creative movement experiences or dances.

Hands-on Thinking. Students who show signs of bodily-kinesthetic intelligence should have opportunities to learn by manipulating objects or by making things with their hands. Many educators have already provided such opportunities by incorporating manipulatives (e.g., Cuisenaire rods, Dienes blocks) into math instruction and involving students in experiments or lab work in science. In thematic projects, too, students use hands-on thinking—for instance, in constructing adobe huts for a unit on Native American traditions or in building dioramas of the rain forest for an ecology theme. You can extend this general strategy into many other curricular areas as well. At a rote level, students can study spelling words or new vocabulary words by forming them in clay or with pipe cleaners. At a higher cognitive level, students can express complex concepts by creating clay or wood sculptures, collages, or other assemblages. For example, students could convey an understanding of the term "deficit" (in its economic sense) using only clay (or some other available material) and then share their productions during a class discussion.

Body Maps. The human body provides a convenient pedagogical tool when transformed into a reference point or "map" for specific knowledge domains. One of the most common examples of this approach is the use of fingers in counting and calculating (elaborate finger-counting systems such as "chisanbop" have been adapted for classroom use). We can map out many other domains onto the body. In geography, for example, the body might represent the United States (if the head represents the Northern United States, where is Florida located?). The body can also be used to map out a problem-solving strategy in math. For example, in multiplying a two-digit number by a one-digit number, the feet could be the two-digit number, and the right knee could be the one-digit number. Students could then perform the following actions in "solving" the problem: tap the right knee and the right foot to get the first product (indicated by tapping the thighs); tap the right knee and the left foot to get the second product (indicated by tapping the stomach); tap the thighs and the stomach (to indicate adding the two products), and tap the head (to indicate the final product). By repeating physical movements that represent a specific process or idea, students can gradually internalize the process or idea.

Teaching Strategies for Musical Intelligence

For thousands of years, knowledge was imparted from generation to generation through the medium of singing or chanting. In the 20th century, advertisers have discovered that musical jingles help people remember their client's product. Educators, however, have been slower to recognize the importance of music in learning. As a result, most of us have thousands of commercial musical jingles in our long-term memory but relatively few school-related musical pieces. The following strategies will help you begin to integrate music into the core curriculum:

Rhythms, Songs, Raps, and Chants. Take the essence of whatever you are teaching and put it into a rhythmic format that can be either sung, rapped, or chanted. At a rote level, this can mean spelling words to the rhythm of a metronome or singing the times tables to a popular song. You can also identify the main point you want to emphasize in a lecture, the main idea of a story, or the central theme of a concept, and then place it in a rhythmic format. For example, to teach John Locke's concept of Natural Law, one half of the class can chant "natural law, natural law, natural law, natural law . . ." while the other half repeats: "life, li-ber-ty, happ-i-ness, life, li-ber-ty, happ-i-ness . . ." Inviting students themselves to create songs, raps, or chants that summarize, synthesize, or apply meanings from subjects they are studying moves students to an even higher level of learning. This strategy can also be enhanced through the addition of percussion or other musical instruments.

Discographies. Supplement your bibliographies for the curriculum with lists of recorded musical selections—tapes, compact discs, and records—that illustrate, embody, or amplify the content you want convey. For example, in developing a unit about the Civil War, you could collect songs related to that period in history, including "When Johnny Comes Marching Home Again," "Tenting Tonight," "The Battle Hymn of the Republic," and the more contemporary "The Night They Drove Old Dixie Down." After listening to the recordings, the class can discuss the content of the songs in relation to the themes of the unit.

Additionally, you can find recorded musical phrases, songs, or pieces that sum up in a compelling way the key point or main message of a lesson or unit. For example, to illustrate Newton's first law of motion (A body remains in its state of rest unless it is compelled to change that state by a force impressed on it), you could play the first few lines of Sammy Davis Jr.'s version of "Something's Gotta Give" ("When an irresistible force such as you . . ."). Such "musical concepts" are often effective openers (providing an anticipatory set) to a lesson.

Supermemory Music. Twenty-five years ago, educational researchers in eastern Europe discovered that students could more easily commit information to memory if they listened to the teacher's instruction against a musical background. Baroque and classical musical selections in 4/4 time were found to be particularly effective (e.g., Pachelbel's Canon in D and the Largo movements of concertos by Handel, Bach, Telemann, and Corelli). Students should be in a relaxed state (putting heads on the desk or lying on the floor) while the teacher rhythmically gives the information to be learned (e.g., spelling or vocabulary words, history facts, science terms) against the musical background (see Rose 1987).

Musical Concepts. Musical tones can be used as a creative tool for expressing concepts, patterns, or schemas in many subjects. For example, to convey musically the idea of a circle, begin humming at a certain tone, drop the tone gradually (indicating the gradual slope of the circle) to a low note, and then gradually move up toward the original tone. You can use similar techniques to express cosines, ellipses, and other mathematical shapes. And you can use *rhythms* to express ideas. For example, in a lesson on Shakespeare's *Romeo and Juliet,* you can pit rhythms against each other to suggest the two families in conflict, while in the midst of those rhythms, two quieter rhythms can be heard coming into harmony with each other (the figures of Romeo and Juliet). This strategy offers ample opportunity for creative expression from both teachers and students.

Mood Music. Locate recorded music that creates an appropriate mood or emotional atmosphere for a particular lesson or unit. Such music can even include sound effects (most nonverbal sounds are processed through the musical intellect), nature sounds, or classical or contemporary pieces that facilitate specific emotional states. For example, just before students are about to read a story that takes place near the sea, play a recording of sea sounds (waves crashing up against the shore, sea gulls crying, etc.), or *La Mer* (The Sea) by Claude Debussy. (See Bonny and Savary 1990 for more information on music and the mind.)

Teaching Strategies for Interpersonal Intelligence

Some students need time to bounce their ideas off other people if they are to function optimally in the classroom. These social learners have benefited most from the emergence of cooperative learning. But since all children have interpersonal intelligence to one degree or another, every educator should be aware of teaching approaches that incorporate interaction among people. The following strategies can help tap each student's need for belonging and connection to others.

Peer Sharing. Sharing is perhaps the easiest of the MI strategies to implement. All you need to do is say to students, "Turn to a person near you and share _____." The blank space can be filled with virtually any topic. You might want students to process material just covered in class ("Share a question you have about what I just presented"). Or, you might want to begin a lesson or unit with peer sharing to unlock students' existing knowledge about the topic under study ("Share three things that you know about the early settlers in America"). You may want to set up a "buddy system" so each student shares with the same person each time. Or you may want to encourage students to share with different members of the class so that by the end of the year, each person has formed a sharing pair with every student in the classroom. Sharing periods can be short (thirty seconds) or extended (up to an one hour or more). Peer sharing can also evolve into peer tutoring (one student coaching or teaching specific material to another student) or cross-age tutoring (an older student working with a younger charge in a different class).

People Sculptures. Anytime students are brought together to collectively represent in physical form an idea, a concept, or some other specific learning goal, a *people sculpture exists.* If students are studying the skeletal system, they can build a people sculpture of a skeleton in which each person represents a bone or group of bones. For a unit on inventions, students can create people sculptures of different inventions, complete with moving parts. In algebra class, they can create people sculptures of different equations, each person representing either a number or a function in the equation. Similarly, in language arts, students can build people sculptures to represent spelling words (each person holds up a letter), sentences (each student is a word), or whole paragraphs (each person represents a complete sentence). Assign a student to help "direct" the activity, or let the components of the sculpture organize themselves. The beauty of this approach is in having people represent things that were formerly represented only in books, overheads, or lectures. People sculptures raise learning out of its remote theoretical context and put it into an immediately accessible social setting.

Cooperative Groups. The use of small groups working toward common instructional goals is the core component of the cooperative learning model. Such groups probably work most effectively when they have three to eight members. Students in cooperative groups can tackle a learning assignment in a variety of ways. The group may work collectively on a written assignment, for example, with each member contributing ideas— much as screenwriters work when preparing a television episode. The group may also divide its responsibilities in a number of ways. In one case, the group may assign tasks based upon the structure of the assignment, with one member doing the introduction, another taking care of the middle section, and a another contributing the conclusion. Or groups may use a "jigsaw" strategy and assign each student responsibility for a particular book or subtopic. Alternatively, they may assign different roles among group members, so that one person does the writing, a second reviews the writing for spelling and punctuation errors, a third reads the report to the class, and a fourth leads the ensuing discussion.

Cooperative groups are particularly suitable for MI teaching because they can be structured to include students representing the full spectrum of intelligences. For instance, a group charged with the task of creating a videotaped presentation might include a socially developed student to help organize the group, a linguistically inclined member to do the writing, a spatially oriented student to do the drawing, a bodily-kinesthetic student to create props or be a leading actor, and so forth. Cooperative groups provide students with a chance to operate as a social unit—an important prerequisite for successful functioning in real-life work environments.

Board Games. Board games are a fun way for students to learn in the context of an informal social setting. On one level, students are chatting, discussing rules, throwing dice, and laughing. On another level, however, they are engaged in learning whatever skill or subject happens to be the focus of the game. Board games can be easily made using manila file folders, magic markers (to create the typical winding road or path), a pair of dice, and miniature cars, people, or colored cubes (available at toy stores or teacher supply stores) to serve as game pieces. Topics can include a wide range of subjects, from math facts and phonics skills to rain forest data and history questions. The information to be learned can be placed on the individual squares of the winding road (e.g., the math fact 5 x 7) or on cards made from tag board or thick construction paper. Answers can be provided in a number of ways: on a separate answer key, from a specially designated "answer person," or on the board squares or cards themselves (glue a tiny piece of folded paper to each square; on the top flap write the question or problem and on the bottom flap, the answer; players then simply open the flap to read the answer).

You can also design board games that involve quick open-ended or activity-oriented tasks. Simply place the directions or tasks on each square or card (e.g., "Explain what you would do to control pollution if you were president of the United States" or "Look up the word 'threshold' in the dictionary").

Simulations. A simulation involves a group of people coming together to create an "as-if" environment. This temporary setting becomes the context for getting into more immediate contact with the material being learned. For example, students studying a historical period might actually dress up in costumes of that time, turn the classroom into a place that might have existed then, and begin acting *as if* they were living in that era. Similarly, in learning about geographical regions or ecosystems, students could turn the classroom into a simulated jungle or rain forest.

Simulations can be quick and improvisational in nature, with the teacher providing an instant scenario to act out: "Okay, you've just got off the boat on your trip to the New World and you're all standing around together. Begin the action!" Or they can be ongoing and require substantial preparation, such as props, costumes, and other paraphernalia to support the illusion of a particular era or region of the world.

Although this strategy involves several intelligences (including bodily-kinesthetic, linguistic, and spatial), it is included in the interpersonal section because the human interactions that take place help students develop a new level of understanding. Through conversation and other interactions, students begin to get an insider's view of the topic they are studying.

Teaching Strategies for Intrapersonal Intelligence

Most students spend about six hours a day, five days a week in a classroom with twenty-five to thirty-five other people. For individuals with strongly developed intrapersonal intelligence, this intensely social atmosphere can be somewhat claustrophobic. Hence, teachers need to build in frequent opportunities during the day for students to experience themselves as autonomous beings with unique life histories and a sense of deep individuality. Each of the following strategies helps accomplish this aim in a slightly different way:

One-Minute Reflection Periods. During lectures, discussions, project work, or other activities, students should have frequent "time outs" for introspection or deep thinking. One-minute reflection periods offer students time to digest the information presented or to connect it to happenings in their own lives. They also provide a refreshing change of pace that helps students stay alert and ready for the next activity.

A one-minute reflection period can occur anytime during the school day, but it may be particularly useful after the presentation of information that is especially challenging or central to the curriculum. During this one-minute period (which can be extended or shortened to accommodate differing attention spans), there is to be no talking and students are to simply think about what has been presented in any way they'd like. Silence is usually the best environment for reflection, but you occasionally might want to use background "thinking" music. Also, students should not feel compelled to "share" what they thought about, but asking whether any students wish to share their thoughts with the class can be useful.

Personal Connections. The big question that accompanies strongly intrapersonal students through their school career is: "What does all this have to do with *my* life?" Most students have probably asked this question in one way or another during their time in school. It's up to teachers to help answer this question by continually making connections between what is being taught and the lives of their students. This strategy, then, asks you to weave students' personal associations, feelings, and experiences into your instruction. You may do so through questions ("How many of you have ever . . . ?"), statements ("You may wonder what this has to do with your lives. Well, if you ever plan on . . ."), or requests ("I'd like you to think back in your life to a time when . . ."). For instance, to introduce a lesson on the skeletal system, you might ask, "How many people here have ever broken a bone?" Students then share stories and experiences before going on to the anatomy lesson itself. Or, for a lesson on world geography, you might ask, "Has anybody every been to another country? What country?" Students then identify the countries they've visited and locate them on the map.

Choice Time. Giving students choices is as much a fundamental principle of good teaching as it is a specific intrapersonal teaching strategy. Essentially, choice time consists of building in opportunities for students to make decisions about their learning experiences. Making choices is like lifting weights. The more frequently students choose from a group of options, the thicker their "responsibility muscles" become. The choices may be small and limited ("You can choose to work on the problems on page 12 or 14") or they may be significant and open-ended ("Select the kind of project you'd like to do this semester"). Choices may be related to content ("Decide which topic you'd like to explore") or to process ("Choose from this list a method of presenting your final project"). Choices may be informal and spur-of-the-moment ("Okay, would you rather stop now or continue talking about this?") or they may be carefully developed and highly structured (as in the use of a learning contract for each student). How do you provide for choice in your classroom? Think of ways to expand the choice-making experiences your students can have in school.

Feeling-Toned Moments. One of the sadder findings of John Goodlad's (1984) "A Study of Schooling" was that most of the 1,000 classrooms observed had few experiences of true feeling—that is, expressions of excitement, amazement, anger, joy, or caring. All too often, teachers present information to students in an emotionally neutral way. Yet it's known that human beings possess an "emotional brain" consisting of several subcortical structures (see Holden 1979). To feed that emotional brain, educators need to teach with feeling. This strategy, then, suggests that educators are responsible for creating moments in teaching where students laugh, feel angry, express strong opinions, get excited about a topic, or feel a wide range of other emotions. You can help create feeling-toned moments in a number of ways: first, by modeling those emotions yourself as you teach; second, by making it safe for students to have feelings in the classroom (giving permission, discouraging criticism, and acknowledging feelings when they occur); and finally, by providing experiences (such as movies, books, and controversial ideas) that evoke feeling-toned reactions.

Goal-Setting Sessions. One of the characteristics of highly developed intrapersonal learners is their capacity to set realistic goals for themselves. This ability certainly has to be among the most important skills necessary for leading a successful life. Consequently, educators help students immeasurably in their preparation for life when they provide opportunities for setting goals. These goals may be short-term ("I want everybody to list three things they'd like to learn today") or long-term ("Tell me what you see yourself doing twenty-five years from now"). The goal-setting sessions may last only a few minutes or they may involve in-depth planning over several months' time. The goals themselves can relate to academic outcomes ("What grades are you setting for yourself this term?"), wider learning outcomes ("What do you want to know how to do by the time you graduate?"), or life goals ("What kind of occupation do you see yourself involved with after you leave school?"). Try to allow time *every day* for students to set goals for themselves. You may also want to show students different ways of representing those goals (through words, pictures, etc.) and methods for charting their progress along the way (through graphs, charts, journals, and time lines).

For Further Study

1. Select three strategies from this chapter that intrigue you and that you haven't already used in your classroom. Do background reading or consult with colleagues as needed, and develop specific lesson plans that describe exactly how you will apply the strategies. Try out your lessons and then evaluate the results. What worked and what didn't work? How would you modify each strategy in the future to make it more successful?

2. Choose an intelligence that you usually don't address in your instruction, and research related strategies to use in your teaching (consult the list of strategies in Chapter 5 and the resources list in Appendix B for more sources of ideas).

3. Develop a broad learning experience for your students that incorporates at least one of the strategies for each intelligence in this chapter.

For instance, develop a unit that involves body sculptures, mood music, feeling-toned moments, peer sharing, brainstorming, color coding, and quantifications and calculations. Work alone or as part of an interdisciplinary team.

7 MI and the Classroom Environment

> Nowhere else [but in schools] are large groups of individuals packed so closely together for so many hours, yet expected to perform at peak efficiency on difficult learning tasks and to interact harmoniously.
>
> —Carol Weinstein (1979)

FOR MOST AMERICANS, THE WORD "CLASSROOM" conjures up an image of students sitting in neat rows of desks facing the front of the room, where a teacher either sits at a large desk correcting papers or stands near a blackboard lecturing to students. This is certainly one way to organize a classroom, but it is by no means the only way or the best way. The theory of multiple intelligences suggests that the classroom environment—or classroom *ecology*, if you will—may need to be fundamentally restructured to accommodate the needs of different kinds of learners.

MI and Ecological Factors in Learning

At a minimum, MI theory provides a template through which educators can view some of the critical ecological factors in learning. Each intelligence, in fact, provides a context for asking some hard questions about those factors in the classroom that promote or interfere with learning, and those elements absent from the room that could be incorporated to facilitate student progress. A review of the seven intelligences reveals some of the following questions:

Linguistic Intelligence

• How are spoken words used in the classroom? Are the words used by the teacher too complex or too simple for the students' level of understanding, or is there a good match?

• How are students exposed to the written word? Are words represented on the walls (through posters, quotations, etc.)? Are written words presented through primary sources (e.g., novels, newspapers, historical documents) or through textbooks and workbooks written by committees?

• Is there too much "linguistic pollution" in class (endless exposure to dittos and busy work), or are students being empowered to develop their own linguistic materials?

Logical-Mathematical Intelligence

• How is time structured in the classroom? Do students have opportunities to work on long-term projects without being interrupted, or must they continually break off their activities to move on to a new topic?

• Is the school day sequenced to make optimum use of students' attention spans (morning best for focused academic work, afternoon best for more open-ended activities), or do students have to perform under conditions that don't match changes in their attention span?

• Is there some consistency to students' school days (e.g., routines, rituals, rules, effective transitions to new activities), or is there a sense of chaos, of reinventing the wheel with the start of each new school day?

Spatial Intelligence

• How is the classroom furniture arranged? Are there different spatial configurations to accommodate different learning needs (e.g., desks for written work, tables for discussion or hands-on work, carrels for independent study), or is there only one arrangement (e.g., straight rows of desks)?

• Is the room attractive to the eye (e.g., artwork on the walls, plants on the window sills), or is it visually boring or disturbing?

• Are students exposed to a variety of visual experiences (e.g., optical illusions, cartoons, illustrations, movies, great art), or does the classroom environment function as a visual desert?

• Do the colors of the room (walls, floors, ceiling) stimulate or deaden students' senses?

• What kinds illumination are used (fluorescent, incandescent, natural)? Do the sources of light refresh students or leave them feeling distracted and drained?

• Is there a feeling of spaciousness in the learning environment, or do students feel stressed in part due to overcrowding and lack of privacy?

Bodily-Kinesthetic Intelligence

• Do students spend most of their time sitting at their desks with little opportunity for movement, or do they have frequent opportunities to get up and move around (e.g., through exercise breaks and hands-on activities)?

• Do students receive healthy snacks and a well-designed breakfast or lunch during the day to keep their bodies active and their minds alert, or do they eat junk food during recess and have mediocre cafeteria meals?

• Are there materials in the classroom that allow students to manipulate, build, be tactile or in other ways gain hands-on experience, or does a "don't touch" ethos pervade the room?

Musical Intelligence

• Does the auditory environment promote learning (e.g., background music, white noise, pleasant environmental sounds, silence), or do disturbing noises frequently interfere with learning (e.g., loud buzzers or bells, aircraft overhead, car and truck noises outside, industrial machines)?

• How does the teacher use his or her voice? Does it vary in intensity, inflection, and emphasis, or does it have a dull monotone quality that puts students to sleep?

Interpersonal Intelligence

• Does an atmosphere of belonging and trust permeate the classroom, or do students feel alienated, distant, or mistrustful of one another?

• Are there established procedures for mediating conflict between class members, or must problems often be referred to a higher authority (e.g., the principal) for resolution?

• Do students have frequent opportunities to interact in positive ways (e.g., peer teaching, discussions, group projects, cooperative learning, parties), or are students relatively isolated from one another?

Intrapersonal Intelligence

• Do students have opportunities to work independently, develop self-paced projects, and find time and space for privacy during the day, or are they continually interacting?

• Are students exposed to experiences that heighten their self-concept (e.g., self-esteem exercises, genuine praise and other positive reinforcement, frequent success experiences in their school work), or are they subjected to put-downs, failures, and other negative experiences?

• Do students have the opportunity to share feelings in the classroom, or is the inner life of a student considered off limits?

• Are students with emotional difficulties referred to professional counselors for support, or are they simply left to fend for themselves?

• Are students given authentic choices in how they are to learn, or do they have only two choices: "My way or the highway"?

The answers to the above questions will provide a telling commentary on the quality of the learning environment available to students. If answers consistently tilt toward the negative side of the ecology ledger, then learning is apt to be significantly impaired, even if students come into the classroom as willing, able, and excited learners. On the other hand, answers that veer toward the positive factors listed will enhance a classroom environment to the point where even students who enter the room with significant academic, emotional, or cognitive difficulties will have an opportunity to make great strides in their learning.

MI Activity Centers

In addition to the kinds of general ecological factors described above, there are more specific applications of MI theory to the classroom environment. These focus upon organizing the classroom in such a way that areas of the room are dedicated to specific intelligences. Although students can certainly engage in MI activities while seated at their desks, the use of long periods of seat time places significant limits on the *kinds* of MI experiences they can have. Restructuring the classroom to create "intelligence-friendly" areas or activity centers can greatly expand the parameters for student exploration in each domain.* Activity centers can take a variety

---

*Write Harvard Project Zero (323 Longfellow Hall, Cambridge, MA 02138) for information about Project Spectrum's use of activity centers for preschool children, and New Horizons for Learning (4649 Sunnyside North, Seattle, WA 98103) for information about Bruce Campbell's use of MI activity centers at the elementary school level.

of forms, as illustrated in Figure 7.1. This figure shows MI activity centers existing on two continua, from permanent to temporary centers (Axis A) and from open-ended to topic-specific centers (Axis B).

Permanent Open-Ended Activity Centers

Quadrant 1 of Figure 7.1 represents permanent (usually year-long) centers designed to provide students a wide range of open-ended experiences in each intelligence. Here are some examples of such centers for each intelligence (with some suggested items for each center included in parentheses):

Linguistic Centers
- Book nook or library area (with comfortable seating)
- Language lab (cassettes, earphones, talking books)
- Writing center (typewriters, word processors, paper)

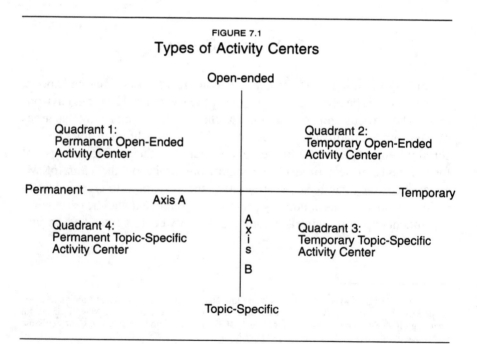

FIGURE 7.1
Types of Activity Centers

Open-ended

Quadrant 1:
Permanent Open-Ended
Activity Center

Quadrant 2:
Temporary Open-Ended
Activity Center

Permanent ——————————————————————— Temporary
Axis A

Quadrant 4:
Permanent Topic-Specific
Activity Center

A
x
i
s

B

Quadrant 3:
Temporary Topic-Specific
Activity Center

Topic-Specific

Logical-Mathematical Centers
• Math lab (calculators, manipulatives)
• Science center (experiments, recording materials)

Spatial Centers
• Art area (paints, collage materials)
• Visual media center (videotapes, slides, computer graphics)
• Visual-thinking area (maps, graphs, visual puzzles, picture library, three-dimensional building materials)

Bodily-Kinesthetic Centers
• Open space for creative movement (mini-trampoline, juggling equipment)
• Hands-on center (clay, carpentry, blocks)
• Tactile-learning area (relief maps, samples of different textures, sandpaper letters)
• Drama center (stage for performances, puppet theater)

Musical Centers
• Music lab (cassettes, earphones, music tapes)
• Music performance center (percussion instruments, tape recorder, metronome)
• Listening lab ("sound" bottles, stethoscope, walkie-talkies)

Interpersonal Centers
• Round table for group discussions
• Desks paired together for peer teaching
• Social area (board games, comfortable furniture for informal social gatherings)

Intrapersonal Centers
• Study carrels for individual work
• Loft (with nooks and crannies for individuals to "hide" in and get away from people)
• Computer hutch (for self-paced study)

Clear labeling of each of these activity centers with explicit MI nomenclature (e.g., "Linguistic Intelligence Center" or "Picture Smart Center") will reinforce students' understanding of MI theory. You may want to explain that the centers are named for the intelligence that is used *most* in each center; intelligences are always interacting, so students don't have to switch activity centers if, for example, they want to add a picture to the writing they're doing in the Word Smart Center.

Temporary Topic-Specific Activity Centers

In Quadrant 3 of Figure 7.1, diagonally across from Quadrant 1, are topic-specific activity centers that change frequently and are geared toward a particular theme or subject. For example, if students are studying a unit on housing, you may create seven different activity centers or "task stations" that involve students in meaningful activities within each intelligence. The activities for the housing unit might include the following:

Linguistic Center: A "Reading Center" where students read books on houses and write about what they read.

Logical-Mathematical Center: A "Computing Center" where students compare the costs, square footage, or other statistical measurements of different houses.

Spatial Center: A "Drawing Center" where students can design and draw a futuristic house.

Bodily-Kinesthetic Center: A "Building Center" where students create a model of a house using balsa wood and glue.

Musical Center: A "Music Center" where students listen to songs about dwellings (e.g., "This Old House" and "We All Live in a Yellow Submarine") and make up their own songs.

Interpersonal Center: An "Interaction Center" where students "play house" (simulate a home environment with peers).

Intrapersonal Center: An "Experience Center" where students think, write, draw, and act out their personal experiences with the homes they've lived in or with an image of their own dream house.

Temporary Open-Ended Activity Centers

Quadrant 2 of Figure 7.1 represents activity centers for open-ended exploration that can be set up and taken down quickly by a classroom teacher. This type of center can be as simple as having seven tables scattered around the classroom, each clearly labeled with an intelligence and holding intelligence-specific materials that invite students into open-ended activities. Games lend themselves particularly well to temporary open-ended activity centers. Here are some examples:

- *Linguistic Center:* Scrabble
- *Logical-Mathematical Center:* Monopoly
- *Spatial Center:* Pictionary
- *Bodily-Kinesthetic Center:* Twister
- *Musical Center:* Simon
- *Interpersonal Center:* Family Feud
- *Intrapersonal Center:* The Ungame

Temporary open-ended activity centers are especially useful for introducing students to the idea of multiple intelligences and for giving them quick experiences that illustrate the intelligences.

Permanent Topic-Specific (Shifting) Activity Centers

Finally, Quadrant 4 of Figure 7.1 represents activity centers that are essentially a combination of Quadrant 1 (ongoing and permanent) and Quadrant 3 (topic-specific and temporary) activity centers. Permanent topic-specific activity centers are most appropriate for teachers working with year-long themes along the lines of Susan Kovalik's (1993) Integrated Thematic Instruction (ITI) model. Each center exists year-round and has a number of materials and resources that never change (e.g., art supplies in the Spatial Center and hands-on materials in the Bodily-Kinesthetic Center). Within each center, however, are revolving "explorations" that change with every monthly component or weekly topic of the year-long theme. So, for example, if the year-long theme is "Change" (more appealingly titled "Does Everything Change?"), a month-long component might deal with the seasons, and weekly topics might focus on individual seasons. The activity centers, then, focus on winter for one week, then shift to spring the next week, and to summer and fall in subsequent weeks. Every center might have activity cards posted that tell students what kinds of things they can work on either alone or cooperatively. For example, the activity cards for the topic of "summer" might read as follows:

Linguistic Center: "Write a poem about what you plan to do during the summer. If this is a cooperative group activity, first choose a scribe to write down the poem. Then each person contribute a line to the poem. Finally, choose someone to read the poem to the class."

Logical-Mathematical Center: "First find out how many days there are in your summer vacation. Then figure how out many minutes are in that number of days. Finally, calculate the number of seconds in your summer vacation. If this is a group activity, collaborate with the other members of your group on your answers."

Spatial Center: "Make a drawing of some of the things you plan to do during the summer. If this is a group activity, do a group drawing on a long sheet of mural paper."

Bodily-Kinesthetic Center: "Create your own representation of 'summer' out of a piece of clay. If this is a group activity, cooperate with the other members of your group to create a clay sculpture or quickly improvise a short play that includes the group's favorite summer activities."

Musical Center: "Make up a rap or song about summer. If this is a group activity, collaborate on a group song to sing to the class, or brainstorm all the songs you can think of that have to do with summer and be prepared to sing some of them to the class."

Interpersonal Center: "Have a group discussion about what you think makes for a *great* summer and select a spokesperson to summarize your conclusions in front of the class."

Intrapersonal Center: "Make a list or a series of sketches of all the things you like about summer." [*Note:* students work alone in this center.]

Student Choice and Activity Centers

Should students be able to choose which activity centers they work in? The answer to this question may depend upon the type of activity center (which quadrant) and the purpose of each center. Generally speaking, Quadrant 1 and 2 activity centers (those involving open-ended experiences) are best structured as "choice" activities. In other words, you can make them available to students during break times, recess, or special "choice times" after students have completed their other schoolwork. When used in this way, activity centers provide excellent assessment information about students' "proclivities" in the seven intelligences. Students usually gravitate toward activity centers based on intelligences in which they feel most competent. For example, students who repeatedly go to the "Picture Smart" area and engage in drawing activities are sending a strong message to the teacher about the importance of visual representation in their lives.

Quadrant 3 and Quadrant 4 activity centers emphasize directed study. Consequently, when using these types of centers, you may want to let students choose the activity center they would like to *start* with but then have everyone rotate center by center in a clockwise manner until everyone has had experience in all seven centers. Using this rotation system from time to time with Quadrant 1 and 2 activity centers will ensure that students have experiences across the wide spectrum of intelligences.

Activity centers provide students with the opportunity to engage in "active" learning. They serve as oases in the desert for many students who are thirsting for something other than dry worksheets and individual work at their desks. MI theory allows you to structure activity centers in ways that activate a wide range of learning potentials in students. Though the descriptions above have been limited to centers based on individual intelligences, there is no reason that centers can't be structured to combine intelligences in different ways. In this sense, virtually any activity center that goes beyond simple reading, writing, or calculation activities qualifies as an MI center. A "Naturalist's Center" combining logical-mathematical and bodily-kinesthetic intelligences or a "Composer's Corner" combining linguistic and musical intelligences are just two examples of MI centers that combine intelligences.

For Further Study

1. Survey your classroom environment using the questions on pages 86–89 as a guide. List the changes you would like to make in the ecology of your classroom. Prioritize them (putting those items that you'd like to change, but can't, on a separate list). Then set about making those changes you *can* make one at a time.

2. Set up MI activity centers in your classroom. First, decide which type of activity center you'd like to start out with (i.e., centers in Quadrant 1, 2, 3, or 4). Then list the materials you need and create a schedule for setting up the centers. Enlist the help of parent volunteers or colleagues if necessary.

If you have established permanent centers, assess the project after two or three weeks of use. If you have established temporary centers, assesses their success immediately after students' experience with them. Use your self-evaluation to guide the design of future centers.

3. To introduce the idea of activity centers to your class, select a topic that has an emotional charge and that everyone has had some experience with—for instance, "fast food." Put up seven signs at various points around the room, each bearing the symbol for an intelligence. Under each sign, tape a "task card." Then signal students to move toward the intelligence that they feel most comfortable with (make sure they've been introduced to MI in some way before this activity; see Chapter 3 for ideas). Students then read the task for their area and cooperatively begin working on it. Set a time to reconvene so the groups can present their findings. Suggestions for tasks related to the topic of "fast food" include:

• *Linguistic Task:* "Create a poem about fast food."

• *Logical-Mathematical Task:* "Using the nutritional charts provided by the fast-food outlets you see here, develop a fast-food meal menu that is as low in fat as possible; then put together a fast-food menu that is as high in fat as possible."

• *Spatial Task:* "Create a mural that deals with people's fast-food eating habits."

• *Bodily-Kinesthetic Task:* "Rehearse a role play or commercial (with or without words) about people's fast-food eating habits and then present it to the class."

• *Musical Task:* "Write a jingle or a rap about people's fast-food eating habits and then sing it together."

• *Interpersonal Task:* "Discuss among yourselves the fast-food eating habits of your small group, and then go out and canvas the rest of the class about their fast-food eating habits. Select a scribe to record and report the results."

• *Intrapersonal Task:* "Think about these questions: If you could be any fast food, which would you be? Why? Choose a method for recording your thoughts (e.g., drawing, writing, or pantomime). You may work alone or as a group."

8 MI and Classroom Management

Nature endows a child with a sensitiveness to order. It is a kind of inner sense that distinguishes the relationships between various objects rather than the objects themselves. It thus makes a whole of an environment in which the several parts are mutually dependent. When a person is oriented in such an environment, he can direct his activity to the attainment of specific goals. Such an environment provides the foundation for an integrated life.

—Maria Montessori (1972, p. 55)

A CLASSROOM IS A MICROSOCIETY COMPLETE with student citizens, many of whom have competing needs and interests. Consequently, rules, routines, regulations, and procedures are a fundamental part of the classroom infrastructure. MI theory, while not providing a classroom management scheme per se, offers beleaguered teachers a new perspective on the many kinds of management strategies that they have used to "keep the peace" and ensure a smoothly running learning environment.

Gaining Students' Attention

Perhaps the best illustration of MI theory's utility in the area of classroom management can be seen in the ways in which teachers have sought to gain their students' attention at the beginning of a class or a new learning activity. A comedy record some years ago humorously recounted one teacher's attempts to bring her class to order. Against the loud hum of student noise, the teacher loudly said: "Class!" This not working, she upped the voltage somewhat: "Class!!" And once more, even more loudly: "Class!!!" Seeing her ineffectiveness, she finally screamed: "SHUT UP!!!!" And the class became quiet. But then the talking started

97

again, the noise began to grow, and again she started the same sequence: "Class! . . . Class!! . . . Class!!! . . . SHUT UP!!!!" And once again quiet. The teacher repeated this process several times until the ultimate futility of her attempts became painfully (and laughably) obvious.

Teachers can laugh at this situation because many have had the same experience. From a multiple-intelligence perspective, however, the use of mere words to quiet a class—a *linguistic* approach—might be seen as the *least* effective way to gain the class's attention. Often, the teacher's linguistic requests or commands (as "figure") dissolve in the students' linguistic utterances (as "ground"). Students do not readily differentiate the teacher's voice from the other voices surrounding them. As a result, they fail to attend to directions. This phenomenon is particularly evident among students who have been diagnosed with "attention deficit disorder," but it exists to a certain extent among most students.

A look at some of the more effective techniques used by teachers to grab attention suggests the need to move to other intelligences. So, for example, the kindergarten teacher's playing a piano chord to ask for silence (musical intelligence), the 4th grade teacher's flicking the lights on and off to call the class to attention (spatial intelligence), and the high school teacher's use of silence as an injunction to self-responsibility (intrapersonal intelligence) all demonstrate an understanding of the need to find a nonlinguistic way of gaining students' attention. Here are several other strategies for getting students' attention in the classroom:

Linguistic Strategy: Write the words "Silence, please!" on the blackboard.

Musical Strategy: Clap a short rhythmic phrase and have students clap it back.

Bodily-Kinesthetic Strategy: Put your finger against your lips to suggest silence while holding your other arm up. Have students mirror your gestures.

Spatial Strategy: Put a picture of an attentive classroom on the board and refer to it with a pointer.

Logical-Mathematical Strategy: Use a stopwatch to keep track of the time being wasted and write on the blackboard the number of seconds lost at thirty-second intervals. Let students know that this is time taken away from regular instruction that will need to be made up at a later date.

Interpersonal Strategy: Whisper in the ear of a student, "It's time to start—pass it on," and then wait while students pass the message around the room.

Intrapersonal Strategy: Start teaching the lesson and allow students to take charge of their own behavior.

By looking at these "tricks of the trade" in terms of the theory of multiple intelligences, we discover a fundamental methodology that can be used in structuring other types of classroom routines, such as preparing students for transitions, initiating activities, giving instructions, and forming small groups. Essentially, the underlying mechanism of each of these routines involves cueing students in such a way as to link symbols from one or more of the seven intelligences to specific commands and behaviors. In other words, teachers need to discover ways of cueing students not simply through the spoken word, but through pictures or graphic symbols (spatial), gestures and physical movements (bodily-kinesthetic), musical phrases (musical), logical patterns (logical-mathematical), social signals (interpersonal), and feeling-toned stimuli (intrapersonal).

Preparing for Transitions

To help prepare students for transitions, you can teach the class specific cues and provide a different cue for each type of transition. When focusing on musical intelligence, for example, you could explain that you will use different selections of music to cue different transitions:

- *Get-ready-for-recess music:* Beethoven's *Pastoral* Symphony (Symphony No. 6)
- *Get-ready-for-lunch music:* "Food, Glorious Food" from *Oliver!*
- *Get-ready-for-dismissal music:* "Goin' Home" movement from Dvořák's *New World* Symphony (Symphony No. 9)

If spatial intelligence is your focus, you might use graphic symbols or pictures to signal that it's time to get ready for an event. You might even use photographs or slides of students:

- *Get-ready-for-recess image:* Picture of kids playing
- *Get-ready-for-lunch image:* Kids eating in cafeteria
- *Get-ready-for-dismissal image:* Students getting on the school bus or walking home from school

For bodily-kinesthetic intelligence, you might use specific gestures or body movements to signal the coming event. With this type of strategy, you begin the gesture and students then make the gesture, indicating that they have "received" the message:

- *Get-ready-for-recess gesture:* Stretching and yawning (signifying "time for a break")
- *Get-ready-for-lunch gesture:* Rubbing stomach and licking lips
- *Get-ready-for-dismissal gesture:* Putting hand above eyes and peering outside of the classroom (signifying looking in a homeward direction)

For logical-mathematical intelligence, you could display a large digital "countdown" clock that students can see from anywhere in the classroom, set it for the time left until the transition, and then let students keep track of the time left until the transition occurs. For interpersonal intelligence, you could use a telephone-tree model; simply give the cue to one student, who then tells *two* students, who themselves each tell two students, and so forth, until all students are personally informed.

Communicating Class Rules

You can communicate the school or classroom rules for proper conduct through a multiple-intelligence approach. Some possibilities include:

Linguistic Communication: Rules are written and posted in the classroom (this is the most typical approach).

Logical-Mathematical Communication: Rules are numbered and later referred to by number (e.g., "You just broke rule #4").

Spatial Communication: Next to the written rules are graphic symbols of what to do and what not do to.

Bodily-Kinesthetic Communication: Each rule has a specific gesture; students show they know the rules by going through the different gestures.

Musical Communication: The rules are set to a song (either written by students or set to the melody of an existing song) or each rule is associated with a relevant song.

Interpersonal Communication: Each rule is assigned to a small group of students who then have responsibility for knowing its ins and outs, interpreting it, and even enforcing it.

Intrapersonal Communication: Students are responsible for *creating* the class rules at the beginning of the year and developing their own unique ways of communicating them to others.

Asking students to help create classroom rules is a common way of gaining their support of the rules. Similarly, asking students to help develop their own MI strategies or cues for classroom procedures is a useful way to establish effective cues. Students may want to provide their own music, or create their own gestures, or draw their own graphic symbols to signal the class for different activities, transitions, rules, or procedures.

Forming Groups

Another application of MI theory to classroom management is in the forming of small groups. Although groups have often been formed on the basis of intrinsic factors (e.g., interest/ability groups), educators have increasingly seen the value of heterogeneous groups working cooperatively. MI theory provides a wide range of techniques for creating heterogeneous groups based on incidental features related to each intelligence. Some of the following ideas have been adapted from of the work of Joel Goodman and Matt Weinstein (1980):

Linguistic Strategy: "Think of a vowel sound in your first name. Now make that vowel sound out loud. Go around the room and find three or four people who are making the *same* vowel sound."

Logical-Mathematical Strategy: "When I give the signal, I want you to raise between one and five fingers. . . . Go! Now keep those fingers raised and find three or four people whose raised fingers combined with yours total fifteen."

Spatial Strategy: "Find three or four people who are wearing the same color clothes you are wearing."

Bodily-Kinesthetic Strategy: "Start hopping on one foot. . . . Now find three or four people who are hopping on the same foot."

Musical Strategy: "What are some songs that everybody knows?" The teacher writes on the board four or five of them (e.g., "Row, Row, Row Your Boat," "Happy Birthday to You"). "Okay, I'd like you to file past me while I whisper in your ear one of these songs. Remember which one it is, and when I give the signal, I'd like you to sing your song and find all the others in the class who are singing the same song. . . . Go!"

You need not address *all* intelligences when developing a classroom management scheme. But by reaching beyond the traditional linguistic approach and using some of the other intelligences (two or three at a minimum), you will be providing students with more opportunities for internalizing classroom routines.

Managing Individual Behaviors

Regardless of how effectively you communicate class rules, routines, and procedures, there will always be a few students who—because of biological, emotional, or cognitive differences or difficulties—fail to abide by them. These few students may well take up much of your classroom time as you remind them (through several intelligences!) to sit down, stop throwing things, quit hitting, and start behaving. Although MI theory has no magical answer to their problems (no model does), it can provide a context for looking at a range of discipline systems that have proved effective with difficult behaviors. Naturally, MI theory suggests that no *one* discipline approach is best for all kids; in fact, the theory suggests that teachers need to match different discipline approaches to different kinds of learners. What follows is a broad range of discipline methods matched to the seven intelligences:

Linguistic Discipline Methods
• Talk with the student.
• Provide books for the student that refer to the problem and point to solutions.
• Help the student use "self-talk" strategies for gaining control.
• Tell the student stories that focus on the discipline issue (e.g., "The Boy Who Cried Wolf" for a persistent fibber).

Logical-Mathematical Discipline Methods
• Use Dreikurs' logical-consequences approach (Dreikurs and Soltz 1964).
• Have the student quantify and chart the occurrence of negative and/ or positive behaviors.

Spatial Discipline Methods

• Have the student draw and/or visualize appropriate behaviors.

• Provide the student with a metaphor to use in working with the difficulty (e.g., "If you were an animal, which one would you be?" or "If people say bad things to you, see the bad things as arrows that you can dodge").

• Show the student slides or movies that deal with the issue or that model the appropriate behaviors.

Bodily-Kinesthetic Discipline Methods

• Have the student role play the inappropriate and appropriate behaviors

• Teach the student to use physical cues to deal with stressful situations (e.g., taking a deep breath, tightening and relaxing muscles).

Musical Discipline Methods

• Find musical selections that deal with the issue the student is facing.

• Provide music that reflects the appropriate behavior (e.g., calm music for an out-of-control child).

• Teach the student to "play" his favorite music in his mind when he feels out of control.

Interpersonal Discipline Methods

• Provide peer group counseling.

• Buddy up the student with a role model.

• Have the student teach or look after a younger child.

• Give the student other social outlets for his energies (e.g., leading a group).

Intrapersonal Discipline Methods

• Teach the student to voluntarily go to a nonpunitive "time-out" area to gain control.

• Provide one-to-one counseling.

• Develop a behavior contract.

• Give the student the opportunity to work on high-interest projects.

• Provide self-esteem activities.

Behavioral strategies can be further tailored to the needs of students with specific kinds of difficulties. Figure 8.1 suggests what some of these interventions might look like.

Taking a Broader Perspective

The above strategies, of course, are no substitute for a comprehensive professional team approach to a student's emotional problems or behavioral difficulties. MI theory is valuable, however, because it provides teachers with the means to sort through a broad range of behavioral strategies and discipline systems, and offers guidelines for selecting a limited number of interventions to try out based upon the student's individual differences.

Sometimes the best strategy for a student may be one matched to a poorly developed intelligence. For example, if a student has behavior

FIGURE 8.1

MI Strategies for Managing Individual Behaviors

	Aggressive Student	Withdrawn Student	Hyperactive Student
Linguistic	Bibliotherapy on theme of anger	Introspective novel involving friendship (e.g., *The Secret Garden*)	Books on theme of hyperactivity
Logical-Mathematical	Dreikurs' logical-consequences system	Interactive computer network, chess club, etc.	Quantification of time-on-task
Spatial	Use of metaphor (e.g., favorite animal), visualizing defenses	Movies on theme of withdrawn child who meets a friend	Video games that help develop focus and control
Bodily-Kinesthetic	Role play aggressive behavior and try out alternatives	Pairing with trusted person for walks, sports, games, etc.	Progressive relaxation, yoga, hands-on learning
Musical	Harmonizing music	Energizing music	Soothing, calming music
Interpersonal	Matching with child of similar choleric temperament	Group counseling	Leadership role in cooperative learning group
Intrapersonal	Time-out, contracting	One-to-one counseling/psychotherapy	Quiet-time focusing exercises

problems because of an underdeveloped interpersonal intelligence, then he may benefit most from activities that seek to develop his social skills. In other cases, however, the best strategies will be in a student's areas of strength. For example, you probably would not want to assign reading to a student who has problems with both reading and "acting out" his frustrations. This strategy might only aggravate the situation. On the other hand, helping a student *master* a reading problem may be an important ingredient in improving her classroom behavior. For a student who acquires knowledge easily through the printed word, providing behavioral strategies geared to this strength would, generally speaking, be among the most appropriate choices.

Ultimately, MI theory used in conjunction with classroom management goes far beyond the provision of specific behavioral strategies and techniques. MI theory can greatly affect students' behavior in the classroom simply by creating an environment where individual needs are recognized and attended to throughout the school day. Students are less likely to be confused, frustrated, or stressed out in such an environment. As a result, there is likely far less need for behavioral "tricks" or elaborate discipline systems—which often are initiated only when the learning environment has broken down. As Leslie Hart points out:

> Classroom management, discipline, teacher burn-out, student "failures"—these are all problems inherent in the teacher-does-everything approach. Permit and encourage students to use their brains actively to learn, and the results can be astonishing (Hart 1981, p. 40).

For Further Study

1. Select a classroom routine that students are currently having trouble adapting to (e.g., moving from one activity to another, learning class rules) and experiment with different intelligence-specific cues for helping students master it.

2. Try out nonverbal ways of getting students' attention through musical, spatial, bodily-kinesthetic, interpersonal, logical-mathematical, or intrapersonal intelligences. Develop cues different from those mentioned in this chapter.

3. Choose a student who has been particularly disruptive in class or whose behavior in some other way has proved difficult to handle. Deter-

mine his or her most-developed intelligences (using identification strategies from Chapter 3). Then select behavioral strategies that match the
most-developed intelligences. Consider also strategies in less-developed
intelligences that would help develop skills in areas of need. Evaluate
the results.

4. Review the behavioral systems currently used in your classroom
or school. Identify which specific intelligences are addressed and how
they match or do not match the learning strengths of your students.

5. Identify classroom management issues not specifically discussed
in this chapter and relate MI theory to them in some tangible way. What
are the advantages of using MI theory in handling classroom management
problems? What are its limitations?

9 The MI School

> The school we envision commits itself to fostering students' deep understanding in several core disciplines. It encourages students' use of that knowledge to solve the problems and complete the tasks that they may confront in the wider community. At the same time, the school seeks to encourage the unique blend of intelligences in each of its students, assessing their development regularly in intelligence-fair ways.
>
> —Howard Gardner (1993, p. 75)

THE IMPLICATIONS OF MI THEORY EXTEND far beyond classroom instruction. At heart, the theory of multiple intelligences calls for nothing short of a fundamental change in the way schools are structured.* It delivers to educators everywhere the strong message that students who show up for school at the beginning of each day have the right to be provided with experiences that activate and develop all of their intelligences. During the typical school day, every student should be exposed to courses, projects, or programs that focus on developing each of their intelligences, not just the standard verbal and logical skills that for decades have been exalted above other domains in American education.

---

*Gardner's Harvard Project Zero group is currently collaborating with the Coalition of Essential Schools, Yale's School Development Program, Educational Development Center, and three east coast school districts on the development of ATLAS Communities (Authentic Teaching, Learning, and Assessment for all Students), which will be "break the mold" schools funded by the New American Schools Development Corporation. For more information, write: EDC, 55 Chapel St., Newton, MA 02160.

MI and the Traditional School

In most American schools today, programs that concentrate on the neglected intelligences (musical, spatial, bodily-kinesthetic, interpersonal, intrapersonal) tend to be considered "frill" subjects or at least subjects peripheral to the "core" academic courses. When a school district has a budget crisis, fiscal managers usually don't turn first to the reading and math programs for ways to save money. They begin by eliminating the music program, the art program, and the physical education program (see Viadero 1991). Even when these programs are still operating, they often show the subtle influence of verbal and logical demands. John Goodlad, commenting on observations of schools from his monumental "A Study of Schooling," writes: "I am disappointed with the degree to which arts classes appear to be dominated by the ambience of English, mathematics, and other academic subjects. . . . They did not convey the picture of individual expression and artistic creativity toward which one is led by the rhetoric of forward-looking practice in the field" (Goodlad 1984, p. 220). Goodlad found the phys ed classes similarly flawed: "Anything that might be called a program was virtually nonexistent. Physical education appeared to be a teacher-monitored recess. . . ." (Goodlad 1984, p. 222).

Administrators and others who help structure programs in schools can use MI theory as a framework for making sure that each student has the opportunity *every day* to experience direct interaction with each of the seven intelligences. Figure 9.1 suggests some of the programmatic features that span the seven intelligences in school, including traditional courses, supplementary programs, and extracurricular offerings.

The Components of an MI School

Simply providing students with access to a diverse range of school subjects, however, does not necessarily constitute a multiple-intelligence school. In a recent book on MI theory, Gardner (1993a) sets up his vision of the ideal multiple-intelligence school. In particular, Gardner draws upon two nonschool models in suggesting how MI schools might be structured. First, he sees MI schools based in part on the example of contemporary children's museums. According to Gardner, these environments provide a setting for learning that is hands-on, interdisciplinary, based on real-life contexts, and set in an informal atmosphere that promotes

FIGURE 9.1

MI in Traditional School Programs

Intelligence	Subjects	Supplementary Program	Extracurricular Activities

Linguistic	Reading
	Language Arts
	Literature
	English
	Social sciences
	History
	Most foreign
	  languages
	Speech
		Creative writing lab
		Communication
		  skills
			Debate
			School newspaper
			Yearbook
			Language clubs
			Honor society

Logical-Mathematical	Sciences Mathematics Economics	Thinking skills Computer programming	Science clubs Honor society
Spatial	Art Shop Drafting	Visual-thinking lab Architecture Drawing on the right side of the brain	Photography club Audio-visual staff Chess club
Bodily-Kinesthetic	P.E.	Theater games Martial arts New games	Sports teams Drama Cheerleading
Musical	Music	Orff-Schulwerk programs	Band Orchestra Chorus

Interpersonal	none (done at
	  recess and before
	  and after school)
		Social skills
		AIDS/drugs/race
		  awareness
		  programs
			Glee club
			Student government

Intrapersonal	none	Self-esteem
		  development
		  programs
			Special-interest
			  clubs

free inquiry into novel materials and situations. Second, he looks to the age-old model of apprenticeships, where masters of a trade oversee ongoing projects undertaken by their youthful protégés.

Gardner suggests that in an MI school, students might spend their mornings working on traditional subjects in nontraditional ways. In particular, Gardner recommends the use of project-centered instruction. Students look in depth at a particular area of inquiry (a historical conflict, a scientific principle, a literary genre) and develop a project (photo essay, experiment, journal) that reflects an ongoing process of coming to grips with the many dimensions of the topic. Students then go into the community during the second part of the day and further extend their understanding of the topics they are studying in school. Younger students, according to Gardner, might regularly go to children's museums, art or science museums, or other places where hands-on exploratory learning and play are encouraged and where interaction with docents and other expert guides takes place. Older students (past 3rd grade) could choose apprenticeships based upon an assessment of their intellectual proclivities, interests, and available resources. They could then spend their afternoons studying with experts in the community in specific arts, skills, crafts, physical activities, or other real-life endeavors.

Fundamental to Gardner's vision of an MI school are the activities of three key members of the school staff, representing functions that are currently absent from most schools. In Gardner's model, every MI school would have staff in these roles:

Assessment Specialist. This staff member is responsible for developing an ongoing "picture" or record of each child's strengths, limitations, and interests in all seven intelligences. Using intelligence-fair assessments, the assessment specialist documents each child's school experience in many ways (through observation, informal assessments, and multimedia documentation) and provides parents, teachers, administrators, and students themselves with an overview of their intellectual proclivities. (See Chapter 10 for an MI perspective on testing and assessment.)

Student-Curriculum Broker. This person serves as a bridge between the student's gifts and abilities in the seven intelligences and the available resources in the school. The student-curriculum broker matches students to specific courses and electives, and provides teachers with information about how particular subjects might best be presented to a student (e.g., through film, hands-on experiences, books, music). This staff member is responsible for maximizing the student's learning potentials, given the particular kinds of materials, methods, and human resources available in the school.

School-Community Broker. This staff person is the link between the student's intellectual proclivities and the resources available in the wider community. A school-community broker should possess a wealth of information about the kinds of apprenticeships, organizations, mentorships, tutorials, community courses, and other learning experiences available in the surrounding geographic area. This person then attempts to match a student's interests, skills, and abilities to appropriate experiences beyond the school walls (e.g., finding an expert cellist to guide a student's burgeoning interest in playing the cello).

Gardner suggests that the creation of such an MI school is far from utopian. Instead, it depends upon the confluence of several factors, including assessment practices that engage students in the actual materials and symbols of each intelligence, curriculum development that reflects real-life skills and experiences, teacher training programs that reflect sound educational principles and that have master teachers working with students committed to the field, and finally, a high level of community involvement from parents, business leaders, museums, and other learning institutions.

A Model MI School: The Key School

Efforts toward building an MI school have already been underway for several years. One school in particular has been singled out by the media and other educators for recognition: the Key School in Indianapolis, Indiana. In 1984, a group of eight Indianapolis public school teachers contacted Howard Gardner for assistance in helping start a new school in the district. Out of their collaboration (as well as the infusion of new educational ideas from the likes of Mihaly Csikszentmihalyi, Elliot Eisner, Ernest Boyer, James MacDonald, and John Goodlad), the Key School was officially born in September 1987 (see Fiske 1988, Olson 1988).

The Key School combines several different features of multiple-intelligence education to create a total learning experience, including the following:

Daily instruction in all seven intelligences. Students at the Key School take classes in traditional subjects (math, science, language arts), but also receive instruction *every day* in physical education, art, music, Spanish, and computers. Compared with schools nationally, students at Key receive four times the exposure to art, music, and physical education than does the average student in the United States. Each child learns to play a musical instrument, starting with the violin in kindergarten.

Schoolwide themes. Each year, the school staff selects three themes (changing at roughly ten-week intervals) to help focus curricular activity.

Themes used in past years include: Connections, Animal Patterns, Changes in Time and Space, Let's Make a Difference—Environmental Focus, Heritage, and Renaissance—Then and Now. During the development of a theme, whole areas of the school may reflect the learning that is going on. For example, during the environmental theme, part of the school was turned into a simulated tropical rain forest. Students select and develop projects for each theme, which they then present to their teachers and peers during special sessions that are videotaped.

"Pods." These are special learning groups that students individually select based upon their interests. Pods are formed around specific disciplines (such as gardening, architecture, or acting) or cognitive pursuits (such as mathematical thinking, problem solving, and "the mind and movement"). Students work with a teacher possessing special competence in the selected area in an apprenticeship-like context that emphasizes mastering real-world skills and knowledge. In the architecture pod, for example, students "adopted" nine houses in the surrounding area and studied the designs of the houses through walking tours and other activities.

"The Flow Room." Students visit the "flow room" in the school several times each week to engage in activities designed to activate their intelligences in open-ended and playful ways (Cohen 1991). Named after Mihaly Csikszentmihalyi's (1990) concept of "flow" (referring to a positive state of intense absorption in an activity), the "flow room" is stocked with scores of board games, puzzles, computer software programs, and other learning materials. Students can choose to participate in any activity available in the room (either alone or with others). A teacher helps facilitate their experience and also observes how individual students interact with the materials (each of which is keyed to a specific intelligence; for instance, the game Otello is linked to spatial intelligence, while Twister is seen primarily as a bodily-kinesthetic activity.

Community Resource Committee. This group, consisting of community representatives from business, the arts, cultural organizations, government, and higher education, puts together weekly programs or assemblies for the entire student population that are based on interdisciplinary themes. Frequently, the topics are tied into the schoolwide themes; for example, if the theme is the Environment, speakers might present information about sewage treatment, forestry, or lobbying for ecological causes.

Heterogeneous Mixed-Aged Grouping. Students who attend the Key School are chosen randomly by a lottery system. Although some students had previously been labeled "learning disabled" and "gifted" and placed in special education programs, no such programs are currently in place at the Key School. Students in any one class have a wide range of ability levels, a factor that is seen to enrich the program through diversity. (See Chapter 11 for a discussion of MI theory and special education.)

Although the Key School is only one of a number of schoolwide (and districtwide) efforts to implement the theory of multiple intelligences, it clearly provides evidence that systemwide restructuring based on MI theory can become reality—and that successful restructuring can be a grass-roots effort. The Key School was not mandated at an administrative level; it is a product of the energy and commitment of eight public school teachers who had a dream about what education could be for their students.

MI Schools of the Future

The Key School experience should by no means be taken as the only way, or even the preferred way, to develop a multiple-intelligence school. There may be as many possible types of MI schools as there are groups of educators, parents, administrators, and community leaders committed to putting MI principles into action. Regardless of how they are structured, MI schools of the future will undoubtedly continue expanding the possibilities for unleashing children's potentials in all intelligences. Perhaps MI schools of the future will look less like schools and more like the real world, with traditional school buildings serving as temporary conduits through which students move on their way to meaningful experiences in the community. Possibly, programs will arise that specialize in the development of one or more of the intelligences—although we must be quick to guard against a "brave new world" of multiple intelligences that could seek to identify a child's strongest intelligences early in life so as to exploit them and channel them prematurely into a small niche that would serve a narrowly segmented society.

Ultimately, what will enrich the development of MI theory is its implementation in interdisciplinary ways that reflect the ever-changing demands of an increasingly complex society. As society changes—and perhaps as we discover new intelligences to help us cope with these changes—MI schools of the future may reflect features that are right now beyond our wildest dreams.

For Further Study

1. Evaluate your school in terms of multiple-intelligence theory. During the course of a school day, does each student have the opportunity to develop each of the seven intelligences for its own sake? Specify programs, courses, activities, and experiences to support your answer to this question. How could the school's programs be modified to incorporate a broader spectrum of intelligences?

2. Assuming you had an unlimited amount of money and resources available to you, develop your version of the "ideal" MI school. What will the physical plant look like? Draw a floor plan of the school to illustrate. What kinds of courses will be offered? What will the function of teachers be? What kinds of experiences will students have? If you wish, develop a scenario of an average student going through a typical day at such a school.

3. Contact schools that are now using multiple-intelligence theory as an overall framework or philosophy, and compare and contrast their different ways of applying the model (for information on schools applying MI theory, write Harvard Project Zero Development Group, Longfellow Hall, Appian Way, Cambridge, MA 02138). Which aspects of each program are applicable to your own school or classroom? Which components are not?

4. Discuss some of the problems that schools might have in implementing MI theory as part of a broader reform movement. How can MI theory best fit into a school's restructuring process? What elements can be included in staff development to improve the chances for this model's success?

10 MI and Assessment

> I believe that we should get away altogether from tests and correlations among tests, and look instead at more naturalistic sources of information about how peoples around the world develop skills important to their way of life.
>
> —Howard Gardner (1987)

THE KINDS OF CHANGES IN INSTRUCTIONAL practice described in the previous nine chapters require an equivalent adjustment in the manner of assessment used to evaluate learning progress. It would certainly be the height of hypocrisy to ask students to participate in a wide range of multispectrum experiences in all seven intelligences, and then require them to show what they've learned through standardized tests that focus narrowly on verbal or logical domains. Educators would clearly be sending a double message to students and to the wider community: "Learning in seven ways is fun, but when it comes to our bottom line—evaluating students' learning progress—we've got to get serious again and test the way we've always tested." Thus, MI theory proposes a fundamental restructuring of the way in which educators assess their students' learning progress. It suggests a system that relies far less on formal standardized or norm-referenced tests and much more on authentic measures that are criterion-referenced, benchmarked, or ipsative (i.e., that compare a student to his or her own past performances).

The multiple-intelligence philosophy of assessment is closely in line with the perspective of a growing number of leading educators who in recent years have argued that authentic measures of assessment probe students' understanding of material far more thoroughly than multiple-choice or fill-in-the-blank tests (see Herman, Aschbacher, and Winters 1992; Wolf, LeMahieu, and Eresh 1992; Gardner 1993a). In particular, authentic measures allow students to show what they've learned *in context*—in other words, in a setting that closely matches the environment in which they would be expected to show that learning in real life. Standardized measures, on the other hand, almost always assess students in artificial settings far removed from the real world. Figure 10.1 lists a number of other ways in which authentic measures prove superior to standardized testing in promoting educational quality.

Varieties of Assessment Experience

Authentic assessment covers a wide range of instruments, measures, and methods. The most important prerequisite to authentic assessment is *observation*. Howard Gardner (1983, 1993a) has pointed out that we can best assess students' multiple intelligences by observing students manipulating the symbol systems of each intelligence. For instance, you might notice how students play a logical board game, how they interact with a machine, how they dance, or how they cope with a dispute in a cooperative learning group. Observing students solving problems or fashioning products in naturalistic contexts provides the best picture of student competencies in the range of subjects taught in school.

The next most important component in implementing authentic assessment is the *documentation* of student products and problem-solving processes. You can document student performance in a variety of ways, including:

Anecdotal Records. Keep a journal with a section for each child, and record important academic and nonacademic accomplishments, interactions with peers and learning materials, and other relevant information about each child.

Work Samples. Have a file for each child that contains samples of the student's work in language arts, math, art, or other areas you are responsible for. The samples can be photocopies if the child wishes to keep the original.

Audio cassettes. Use cassettes to record reading samples (have the student read into a recorder and also tell back the story at the end) and to record a child's jokes, stories, riddles, memories, opinions, and other samples of oral language; also use audio cassettes to document a child's musical ability (singing, rapping, or playing an instrument).

FIGURE 10.1
Standardized Testing Versus Authentic Assessment

Standardized Testing	Authentic Assessment
• Reduces children's rich and complex lives to a collection of scores, percentiles, or grades.	• Gives the teacher a "felt sense" of the child's unique experience as a learner.
• Creates stresses that negatively affect a child's performance.	• Provides interesting, active, lively, and exciting experiences.
• Creates a mythical standard or norm which requires that a certain percentage of children fail.	• Establishes an environment where every child has the opportunity to succeed.
• Pressures teachers to narrow their curriculum to only what is tested on an exam.	• Allows teachers to develop meaningful curricula and assess within the context of that program.
• Emphasizes one-shot exams that assess knowledge residing in a single mind at a single moment in time.	• Assesses on an *ongoing* basis in a way that provides a more accurate picture of a student's achievement.
• Tends to place the focus of interpretation on errors, mistakes, low scores, and other things that children *can't* do.	• Puts the emphasis on a student's *strengths;* tells what they *can* do and what they're *trying* to do.
• Focuses too much importance on single sets of data (i.e., test scores) in making educational decisions.	• Provides *multiple* sources of evaluation that give a more accurate view of a student's progress.
• Treats all students in a uniform way.	• Treats each student as a unique human being.
• Discriminates against some students because of cultural background and learning style.	• Provides a *culture-fair* assessment of a student's performance; gives everyone an equal chance to succeed.
• Judges the child without providing suggestions for improvement.	• Provides information that is *useful* to the learning process.
• Regards testing and instruction as separate activities.	• Regards assessment and teaching as two sides of the same coin.
• Answers are final; students rarely receive an opportunity to revise, reflect, or redo a testing experience.	• Engages the child in a continual process of self-reflection, mediated learning, and revision.
• Provides results that can be fully understood only by a trained professional.	• Describes a child's performance in common-sense terms that can be easily understood by parents, children, and other noneducators.
• Produces scoring materials that students often never see again.	
• Focuses on "the right answer."	• Results in products that have *value* to students and others.
	• Deals with *processes* as much as final products.

continued

FIGURE 10.1 (CONTINUED)
Standardized Testing Versus Authentic Assessment

Standardized Testing	Authentic Assessment
• Places students in artificial learning environments that disturb the natural ecology of learning.	• Examines students in *unobtrusive* ways within the context of their natural learning environments.
• Usually focuses on lower order learning skills.	• Includes higher order thinking skills and important subjective domains (e.g., insight and integrity).
• Encourages extrinsic learning (e.g., learning to pass a test or to get a good score).	• Fosters learning for its own sake.
• Has time limits that constrain many pupils' thinking processes.	• Provides students with the time they need to work through a problem, project, or process.
• Is generally limited to reading, listening, and marking on a piece of paper.	• Involves creating, interviewing, demonstrating, solving problems, reflecting, sketching, discussing, and engaging in many other active learning tasks.
• Generally forbids students to interact.	• Encourages cooperative learning.
• Promotes unhelpful comparisons between children.	• Compares students to their own past performances.

Videotapes. Use videotapes to record a child's abilities in areas that are hard to document in any other way (e.g., acting out a role in a school play, catching a pass in a football game, demonstrating how she fixed a machine), and videotape students presenting projects they've completed.

Photography. Have a camera on hand to snap pictures of things kids have made that might not be preserved (e.g., three-dimensional constructions, inventions, science and art projects).

Student Journal. Students can keep an ongoing journal of their experiences in school, including writing entries, diagrams, doodles, and drawings.

Student-Kept Charts. Students can keep their own records of academic progress on charts and graphs (e.g., number of books read, progress toward an educational objective).

Sociograms. Keep a visual record of student interactions in class, using symbols to indicate affiliation, negative interaction, and neutral contact between class members.

Informal Tests. Create nonstandardized tests to elicit information about a child's ability in a specific area. Focus on building a qualitative picture of the student's understanding of the material rather than devising a method to expose the student's ignorance in a subject.

Informal Use of Standardized Tests. Give standardized tests to individual students, but don't follow the strict administration guidelines. Relax time limits, read instructions to the student, ask the student to clarify responses, provide opportunities to demonstrate answers in pictures, three-dimensional constructions, music, or other ways. Find out what the student really knows; probe errors to find out how the student is thinking. Use the test as a stimulus to engage the student in a dialogue about the material.

Student Interviews. Periodically meet with students to discuss their school progress, their broader interests and goals, and other relevant issues. Keep a record of each meeting in a student's file.

Criterion-Referenced Assessments. Use measures that evaluate students not on the basis of a norm but with respect to a given set of skills—that is, use assessments that tell in concrete terms what the student can and cannot do (e.g., add two-digit numbers with regrouping, write a three-page story on a subject that interests the student).

Checklists. Develop an informal criterion-referenced assessment system simply by keeping a checklist of important skills or content areas used in your classroom and then checking off competencies when students have achieved them (as well as indicating progress toward each goal).

Classroom Maps. Draw up a classroom map (a bird's-eye view of the classroom with all desks, tables, and activity areas indicated) and make copies of it. Each day indicate patterns of movement, activity, and interaction in different parts of the room, writing on the map the names of the students involved.

Calendar Records. Have students keep records of their activities during the day by recording them on a monthly calendar. You can collect the calendars at the end of every month.

MI Assessment Projects

Several projects that have attempted to create models of assessment congruent with the fundamental philosophy of MI theory have been initiated nationwide, many of them under the direction of Howard Gardner and his colleagues at Harvard University's Project Zero. These include projects at the preschool, elementary, middle school, and high school levels (see Gardner 1993a).*

Project Spectrum. This is a preschool program piloted at the Eliot Pearson Children's School at Tufts University in Medford, Massachusetts. The program uses fifteen separate instruments that are themselves rich and engaging activities forming an integral part of the Spectrum curriculum. They include: creative movement experiences (bodily-kinesthetic/musical); a dinosaur board game involving rolling dice, counting moves, and calculating strategies (logical-mathematical); and a storyboard activity that requires students to create a miniature three-dimensional world and then tell a story about it (spatial/linguistic). The program also makes use of art portfolios and teachers' observations of children engaged in activities in the different centers (e.g., the story-telling area, the building center, the naturalist's corner). In addition to looking for "proclivities" in the seven intelligences, teachers assess each student's characteristic "working styles," looking at whether, for example, the child is either confident or tentative, playful or serious, or reflective or impulsive in their way of approaching different learning settings.

Key School. This is an elementary school program that is part of the Indianapolis Public Schools in Indiana. In this program, educators use videotape extensively in their assessment of learning progress. Students are videotaped at the beginning of the year in an interview format where they share their hopes, fears, and goals for the coming year. They are then videotaped at three points during the year as they are presenting their learning projects. Finally, they are taped at year's end to sum up their accomplishments and look ahead to next year. These video portfolios accompany a student through the grades, providing valuable assessment information to parents, teachers, administrators, and the students themselves. (See Chapter 9 for more information on the Key School).

PIFS (Practical Intelligence for School) Units. This program is a middle school infusion curriculum that seeks to help students develop

---

*For more information about these and other Harvard Project Zero projects, write for a materials list to: Project Zero Development Group, Harvard Graduate School of Education, 323 Longfellow Hall, Cambridge, MA 02138.

metacognitive skills and understandings in school-related activities; units include "Choosing a Project," "Finding the Right Mathematical Tools," "Notetaking," and "Why Go to School." Students are evaluated on these units through contextually rich performance-based assessments. For the unit called "Choosing a Project," the assessment tasks include critiquing three proposal plans and providing suggestions for improving the least promising one. For the unit called "Mathematical Tools," the assessment tasks include solving a problem with limited resources and generating other options for developing solutions.

Arts Propel. This is a high school arts program piloted in the Pittsburgh Public Schools in Pennsylvania. The focus is on two elements: (1) *domain projects,* which are a series of exercises, activities, and productions in the visual arts, music, and creative writing designed to develop student sensitivity to compositional features; (2) *processfolios,* which are ongoing collections of students' artistic productions, such as drawings, paintings, musical compositions, and creative writing, from initial idea through rough drafts to final product. Evaluation procedures include self-assessments (requiring student reflection) and teacher assessments that probe students' technical and imaginative skills and their ability to benefit from self-reflection and critique from others.

Assessment in Seven Ways

MI theory provides its greatest contribution to assessment in suggesting multiple ways to evaluate students. The biggest shortcoming of standardized tests is that they require students to show in a narrowly defined way what they've learned during the year. Standardized tests usually demand that students be seated at a desk, that they complete the test within a specific amount of time, and that they speak to no one during the test. The tests themselves usually contain largely linguistic questions or test items that students must answer by filling in bubbles on computer-coded forms.

MI theory, on the other hand, supports the belief that students should be able to show competence in a specific skill, subject, content area, or domain in any one of a variety of ways. And just as the theory of multiple intelligences suggests that any instructional objective can be taught in at least seven different ways, so too does it imply that any subject can be *assessed* in at least seven different ways.

If, for example, the objective is for students to demonstrate an understanding of the character of Huck Finn in the Mark Twain novel, a standardized test might require students to complete the following task on a testing form:

Choose the word that best describes Huck Finn in the novel:
(a) sensitive
(b) jealous
(c) erudite
(d) fidgety

Such an item demands that students know the meanings of each of the four words and that every student's interpretation of Huck Finn coincide with that of the test maker. For instance, although "fidgety" might be the answer the testers are looking for, "sensitive" might actually be closer to the truth, because it touches on Huck's openness to a wide range of social issues. But a standardized test provides no opportunity to explore or discuss this interpretation. Students who are not particularly word-sensitive may know a great deal about Huck Finn, yet not be able to show their knowledge on this test item.

On the other hand, MI theory suggests a variety of ways in which students could demonstrate their understanding:

Linguistic Demonstration. "Describe Huck Finn in your own words, either orally or in an open-ended written format."

Logical-Mathematical Demonstration. "If Huck Finn were a scientific principle, law, or theorem, which one would he be?"

Spatial Demonstration. "Draw a quick sketch showing something you think Huck Finn would enjoy doing that's *not* indicated in the novel."

Bodily-Kinesthetic Demonstration. "Pantomime how you think Huck Finn would act in a classroom."

Musical Demonstration. "If Huck Finn were a musical phrase, what would he sound like or what song would he be?"

Interpersonal Demonstration. "Who does Huck Finn remind you of in your own life (friends, family, other students, TV characters)?"

Intrapersonal Demonstration. "Describe in a few words your personal feelings toward Huck Finn."

By linking Huck Finn to pictures, physical actions, musical phrases, scientific formulas, social connections, and personal feelings, students have more opportunities to use their multiple intelligences to help articulate their understanding. Implied here is the fundamental notion that many students who have mastered the material taught in school may not have the means to show what they've learned if the only setting available for demonstrating competency is a narrowly focused linguistic testing arena. See Figure 10.2 on the next page for other examples of how students can show competence in specific academic subjects.

Using the "seven ways" context described above, students might be assessed in any number of ways:

• Students could be exposed to all seven performance tasks in an attempt to discover the area(s) in which they were most successful.

• Students might be assigned a performance task based upon the teacher's understanding of their most developed intelligences.

• Students themselves could choose the manner in which they'd like to be assessed. Figure 10.3 on page 125 contains a sample form that suggests how students might "contract" to be assessed in a specific subject area.

Assessment in Context

MI theory expands the assessment arena considerably to include a wide range of possible contexts within which a student can express competence in a specific area. It suggests that both the manner of presentation and the method of response will be important in determining a student's competence. If a student learns primarily through pictures, yet is exposed only to the printed word when learning new material, then she will probably not be able to show mastery of the subject. Similarly, if a student is physically oriented (bodily-kinesthetic), yet has to demonstrate mastery through a paper-and-pencil test, then he probably will not be able to externalize what he knows. Figure 10.4 indicates some of the many combinations possible between method of presentation and method of response in structuring assessment contexts.

A look at Figure 10.4 on page 126 shows that typical testing settings for students in American schools take in only one of the forty-nine contexts shown (the one in the upper left corner: "Read a book, *then write a response.*" Yet even the contexts listed in Figure 10.4 are but a fraction

FIGURE 10.2
Examples of the Seven Ways
Students Can Show Their Knowledge About Specific Topics

	Topic:		
	Factors Associated with the South Losing the Civil War	Development of a Character in a Novel	Principles of Molecular Bonding
Linguistic	Give an oral or written report	Do oral interpretation from the novel with commentary	Explain concept verbally or in writing
Logical-Mathematical	Present statistics on dead, wounded, supplies, etc.	Present sequential cause-effect chart of character's development	Write down chemical formulas and show how derived
Spatial	Draw maps of important battles	Develop flow chart or series of sketches showing rise/fall of character	Draw diagrams that show different bonding patterns
Bodily-Kinesthetic	Create 3-D maps of important battles and act them out with miniature soldiers	Act out the role from beginning of novel to end, showing changes	Build several molecular structures with multicolored pop-beads
Musical	Assemble songs of Civil War that point to causal factors	Present development of character as a musical score	Orchestrate a dance showing different bonding patterns (see below)
Interpersonal	Design class simulation of important battles	Discuss underlying motives and moods relating to development	Demonstrate molecular bonding using classmates as atoms
Intrapersonal	Develop their own unique way of demonstrating competency	Relate character's development to one's own life history	Create scrapbook demonstrating competency

of the potential settings that could be structured for assessment purposes. For example, "Listen to a talking book" could be substituted for "Read a book," and "Tell a story" might replace "Write a response" to structure several other assessment contexts. There are also many opportunities for variety even within each of the combinations shown in Figure 10.4. For example, the experience of a student who chooses to "go on a field trip,

FIGURE 10.3

Celebration of Learning
Student Sign-up Sheet

To show that I know _____, **I would like to:**

_____ write a report
_____ do a photo essay
_____ compile a scrapbook
_____ build a model
_____ put on a live demonstration
_____ create a group project
_____ do a statistical chart
_____ develop an interactive computer presentation
_____ keep a journal
_____ record interviews
_____ design a mural
_____ create a discography based on the topic
_____ give a talk
_____ develop a simulation
_____ create a series of sketches/diagrams
_____ set up an experiment
_____ engage in a debate or discussion
_____ do a mind-map
_____ produce a videotape segment
_____ develop a musical
_____ create a rap or song that encompasses the topic
_____ teach it to someone else
_____ choreograph a dance
_____ develop a project not listed above: _____
_____ other: _____

Brief description of what I intend to do:

_____
Signature of Student   Date

_____
Signature of Teacher   Date

FIGURE 10.4

49 MI Assessment Contexts

	Linguistic Task	Logical-Mathematical Task	Spatial Task	Musical Task	Bodily-Kinesthetic Task	Interpersonal Task	Intrapersonal Task
Linguistic Assessment	Read a book, *then write a response.*	Examine a statistical chart, *then write a response.*	Watch a movie, *then write a response.*	Listen to a piece of music, *then write a response.*	Go on a field trip, *then write a response.*	Play a cooperative game, *then write a response.*	Think about a personal experience, *then write a response.*
Logical-Mathematical Assessment	Read a book, *then develop a hypothesis.*	Examine a statistical chart, *then develop a hypothesis.*	Watch a movie, *then develop a hypothesis.*	Listen to a piece of music, *then develop a hypothesis.*	Go on a field trip, *then develop a hypothesis.*	Play a cooperative game, *then develop a hypothesis.*	Think about a personal experience, *then develop a hypothesis.*
Spatial Assessment	Read a book, *then draw a picture.*	Examine a statistical chart, *then draw a picture.*	Watch a movie, *then draw a picture.*	Listen to a piece of music, *then draw a picture.*	Go on a field trip, *then draw a picture.*	Play a cooperative game, *then draw a picture.*	Think about a personal experience, *then draw a picture.*
Bodily-Kinesthetic Assessment	Read a book, *then build a model.*	Examine a statistical chart, *then build a model.*	Watch a movie, *then build a model.*	Listen to a piece of music, *then build a model.*	Go on a field trip, *then build a model.*	Play a cooperative game, *then build a model.*	Think about a personal experience, *then build a model.*
Musical Assessment	Read a book, *then create a song.*	Examine a statistical chart, *then create a song.*	Watch a movie, *then create a song.*	Listen to a piece of music, *then create a song.*	Go on a field trip, *then create a song.*	Play a cooperative game, *then create a song.*	Think about a personal experience, *then create a song.*
Interpersonal Assessment	Read a book, *then share with a friend.*	Examine a statistical chart, *then share with a friend.*	Watch a movie, *then share with a friend.*	Listen to a piece of music, *then share with a friend.*	Go on a field trip, *then share with a friend.*	Play a cooperative game, *then share with a friend.*	Think about a personal experience, *then share with a friend.*
Intrapersonal Assessment	Read a book, *then design your own response.*	Examine a statistical chart, *then design your own response.*	Watch a movie, *then design your own response.*	Listen to a piece of music, *then design your own response.*	Go on a field trip, *then design your own response.*	Play a cooperative game, *then design your own response.*	Think about a personal experience, *then design your own response.*

then build a model" will vary depending on *where* the field trip was taken, *what* kind of mediating experiences were provided during the trip, and *how* the model-building activity was structured. These factors would themselves give rise to a multiplicity of contexts, some of which might be favorable to a student's demonstration of competency (e.g., a field trip to a place the student is interested in or has had prior experience with) and others which might handicap him (e.g., the use of modeling materials the student didn't like or had no familiarity with, or their use in a setting with peers he didn't get along with).

Of course, you do not need to develop forty-nine different assessment contexts for everything you need to evaluate. Figure 10.4 suggests, however, the need to provide students with assessment experiences that include access to a variety of methods of presentation (inputs) and means of expression (outputs). The kinds of assessment experiences that MI theory proposes—particularly those that are project-based and thematically oriented—offer students frequent opportunities to be exposed to several of these contexts at one time (as the Project Zero programs described earlier illustrate). For example, if students are developing a videotape to show their understanding of the effects of pollution on their local community, they may have to read books, do field work, listen to environmental songs, and engage in cooperative activities (inputs) in order to create a video that includes a montage of pictures, music, dialogue, and words (outputs). This complex project provides the teacher with a context-rich document (the video) within which to assess a student's ecological competencies through a variety of intelligences.

MI Portfolios

As students increasingly engage in multiple-intelligence projects and activities, the opportunities for documenting their learning process in MI portfolios expands considerably. In the past decade, portfolio development among reform-minded educators has often been limited to work requiring the linguistic and logical-mathematical intelligences (writing portfolios and math portfolios). MI theory suggests, however, that portfolios ought to be expanded to include, when appropriate, materials from all seven intelligences. Figure 10.5 lists some of the kinds of documents that might be included in an MI Portfolio.

Naturally, the kinds of materials placed in an MI portfolio will depend upon the educational purposes and goals of each portfolio. There are at least five basic uses for portfolios. I call them "The Five C's of Portfolio Development":

1. *Celebration:* To acknowledge and validate students' products and accomplishments during the year.

2. *Cognition:* To help students reflect upon their own work.

3. *Communication:* To let parents, administrators, and other teachers know about students' learning progress.

FIGURE 10.5
What to Put in an MI Portfolio

To document linguistic intelligence:
- Prewriting notes
- Preliminary drafts of writing projects
- Best samples of writing
- Written descriptions of investigations
- Audiotapes of debates, discussions, problem-solving processes
- Final reports
- Dramatic interpretations
- Reading skills checklists
- Audiotapes of reading or storytelling
- Samples of word puzzles solved

To document logical-mathematical intelligence:
- Math skills checklists
- Best samples of math papers
- Rough notes from computations/problem-solving processes
- Final write-ups of science lab experiments
- Photos of science fair projects
- Documentation of science fair projects (awards, photos)
- Piagetian assessment materials
- Samples of logic puzzles or brainteasers solved
- Samples of computer programs created or learned

To document spatial intelligence:
- Photos of projects
- Three-dimensional mockups
- Diagrams, flow charts, sketches, and/or mind-maps of thinking
- Samples or photos of collages, drawings, paintings
- Videotapes of projects
- Samples of visual-spatial puzzles solved

   4. *Cooperation:* To provide a means for groups of students to collectively produce and evaluate their own work.
   5. *Competency:* To establish criteria by which a student's work can be compared to that of other students or to a standard or benchmark.

The checklist in Figure 10.6 can help you clarify some of the uses to which portfolios might be put in the classroom.
   The process of evaluating MI portfolios and other MI performances presents the most challenging aspect of their development. Current reforms in assessment have emphasized the development of benchmarks, holistic

---

To document bodily-kinesthetic intelligence:
- Videotapes of projects and demonstrations
- Samples of projects actually made
- Videos or other records of the "acting out" of thinking processes
- Photos of hands-on projects

To document musical intelligence:
- Audiotapes of musical performances, compositions, collages
- Samples of written scores (performed or composed)
- Lyrics of raps, songs, or rhymes written by student
- Discographies compiled by student

To document interpersonal intelligence:
- Letters to and from others (e.g., writing to obtain information from someone)
- Group reports
- Written feedback from peers, teachers, and experts
- Teacher-student conference reports (summarized/transcribed)
- Parent-teacher-student conference reports
- Peer-group reports
- Photos, videos, or write-ups of cooperative learning projects
- Documentation of community service projects (certificates, photos)

To document intrapersonal intelligence:
- Journal entries
- Self-assessment essays, checklists, drawings, activities
- Samples of other self-reflection exercises
- Questionnaires
- Transcribed interviews on goals and plans
- Interest inventories
- Samples of outside hobbies or activities
- Student-kept progress charts
- Notes of self-reflection on own work

scoring, or other standards by which complex performances and works can be evaluated (see Herman, Aschbacher, and Winters 1992). In my estimation, these devices are best suited only for the *competency* dimension of portfolio development. For the other four components, emphasis should be placed less on comparison and more on student self-evaluation and on *ipsative* measures (assessment that compares a student to his own past performances). Unfortunately, some teachers are using alternative

---

FIGURE 10.6
MI Portfolio Checklist

How will you use the portfolio?

_____ For student self-reflection (Cognition)
_____ As part of regular school evaluation/report card (Competency)
_____ At parent conferences (Communication, Competency)
_____ In IEP/SST meetings (Communication, Competency)
_____ In communicating to next year's teacher(s) (Communication, Competency)
_____ In curricular planning (Competency)
_____ In acknowledging students' accomplishments (Celebration)
_____ In creating cooperative learning activities (Cooperation)
_____ Other:

How will it be organized?

_____ Only finished pieces from a variety of subjects
_____ Different expressions of a specific objective
_____ Charting of progress from first idea to final realization
_____ Representative samples of a week/month/year's work
_____ Only "best" work
_____ Include "group" work
_____ Other:

What procedures will you use in placing items in the portfolio?

_____ Select regular times for pulling student work
_____ Train students to select (e.g., flagging with stickers)
_____ Pull items that meet preset criteria
_____ Random approach
_____ Other:

What will the portfolio look like?

_____ Two pieces of posterboard stapled or taped together.
_____ Box or other container
_____ Scrapbook
_____ Diary or journal

assessment techniques to reduce students' rich and complex works to holistic scores or rankings like these: Portfolio A is a 1, Portfolio B a 3; Child C's art project is at a "novice" level, while Child D's project is ata "mastery" level. This reductionism ends up looking very much like standardized testing in some of its worst moments. I suggest that we instead initially focus our attention in MI assessment on looking at individual students' work *in depth* in terms of the unfolding of each student's

---

_____ Manila folder
_____ Bound volume
_____ CD-ROM
_____ Other:

Who will evaluate the portfolio?

_____ Teacher alone
_____ Teacher working in collaboration with other teachers
_____ Student self-evaluation
_____ Peer evaluation
_____ Other:

How will the works in the portfolio be arranged?

_____ Chronologically
_____ By student: from "crummy" to "great" (with reasons given)
_____ By teacher: from poor to superior (with reasons given)
_____ From birth of an idea to its fruition
_____ By subject area
_____ Other:

What factors will go into evaluating the portfolio?

_____ Number of entries
_____ Range of entries
_____ Degree of self-reflection demonstrated
_____ Improvement from past performances
_____ Achievement of preset goals (student's, teacher's, school's)
_____ Interplay of production, perception, and reflection
_____ Responsiveness to feedback/mediation
_____ Depth of revision
_____ Group consensus (among teachers)
_____ Willingness to take a risk
_____ Development of themes
_____ Use of benchmarks or standards for comparison
_____ Other:

uniqueness (for appropriate assessment models of this kind, see Carini 1979, 1982, Engel 1977, and Armstrong 1980).

Ultimately, MI theory provides an assessment framework within which students can have their rich and complex lives acknowledged, celebrated, and nurtured. Because MI assessment and MI instruction represent flip sides of the same coin, MI approaches to assessment are not likely to take more time to implement as long as they are seen as an integral part of the instructional process. As such, assessment experiences and instructional experiences should begin to appear virtually indistinguishable. Moreover, students engaged in this process should begin to regard the assessment experience not as a gruesome "judgment day" but rather as another opportunity to learn.

For Further Study

1. Choose an educational outcome that you are preparing students to reach, and then develop an MI-sensitive assessment measure that will allow students to demonstrate their competency in a number of ways (i.e., through two or more of the seven intelligences).

2. Help students develop "celebration portfolios" that include elements from several intelligences (see Figure 10.5 for examples of what to put in a portfolio). Develop a set of procedures for selecting material (see Figure 10.6), and a setting within which students can reflect on their portfolios and present them to others.

3. Put on a "Celebration of Learning" fair at which students can demonstrate competencies and show products they've made that relate to the seven intelligences.

4. Focus on one method of documentation that you'd like to explore, develop, or refine (including photography, videotape, audiotape, or electronic duplication of student work) and begin documenting student work using this medium.

5. Keep a daily or weekly diary in which you record your observations of students demonstrating competency in each of the seven intelligences.

6. Experiment with the kinds of inputs (methods of presentation) and outputs (methods of expression) you use in constructing assessments. Use Figure 10.4 as a guide in developing a variety of assessment contexts.

7. Develop an *ipsative* assessment approach (i.e., one that compares a student to his own past performance) and compare its usefulness to other methods of assessment and evaluation (e.g., standardized tests, benchmarked performances, holistically scored portfolios, etc.).

11 MI and Special Education

Treat people as if they were what they ought to be, and you help them to become what they are capable of being.

—Goethe

THE THEORY OF MULTIPLE INTELLIGENCES has broad implications for special education. By focusing on a wide spectrum of abilities, MI theory places "disabilities" or "handicaps" in a broader context. Using MI theory as a backdrop, educators can begin to perceive children with special needs as whole persons possessing strengths in many intelligence areas. Over the history of the special education movement in the United States, educators have had a disturbing tendency (gifted educators excepted) to work from a deficit paradigm—focusing on what students *can't* do—in an attempt to help students succeed in school. As an example of this trend, Mary Poplin in her farewell address to her readership as editor of the *Learning Disability Quarterly* (LDQ) stated:

> The horrifying truth is that in the four years I have been editor of LDQ, only one article has been submitted that sought to elaborate on the talents of the learning disabled. This is a devastating commentary on a field that is supposed to be dedicated to the education of students with average and above average intelligence. . . . Why do we not know if our students are talented in art, music, dance, athletics, mechanical repair, computer programming, or are creative in other nontraditional ways? . . . It is because, like regular educators, we care only about competence in its most traditional and bookish sense— reading, writing, spelling, science, social studies and math in basal texts and worksheets (Poplin 1984, p. 133).

Similar themes could also be identified in other areas of special education, including speech *pathology,* mental *retardation,* emotional *disturbance,* and attention *deficit* disorder, where the very terms themselves strongly suggest the operation of a disease paradigm in each case (see Armstrong 1987).

MI Theory as a Growth Paradigm

We do not have to regard children with special needs primarily in terms of deficit, disorder, and disease. We can instead begin to work within the parameters of a growth paradigm. Figure 11.1 illustrates some

---

FIGURE 11.1
The Deficit Paradigm Versus the Growth Paradigm in Special Education

Deficit Paradigm	Growth Paradigm
• Labels the individual in terms of specific impairment(s) (e.g., ED, BD, EMR, LD).	• Avoids labels; views the individual as an intact person who happens to have a special need.
• Diagnoses the specific impairment(s) using a battery of standardized tests; focuses on errors, low scores, and weaknesses in general.	• Assesses the needs of an individual using authentic assessment approaches within a naturalistic context; focuses on strengths.
• Remediates the impairment(s) using a number of specialized treatment strategies often removed from any real-life context.	• Assists the person in learning and growing through a rich and varied set of interactions with real-life activities and events.
• Separates the individual from the mainstream for specialized treatment in a segregated class, group, or program.	• Maintains the individual's connections with peers in pursuing as normal a life pattern as possible.
• Uses an esoteric collection of terms, tests, programs, kits, materials, and workbooks that are different from those found in a regular classroom.	• Uses materials, strategies, and activities that are good for *all* kids
• Segments the individual's life into specific behavioral/educational objectives that are regularly monitored, measured, and modified.	• Maintains the individual's integrity as a whole human being when assessing progress toward goals.
• Creates special education programs that run on a track parallel with regular education programs; teachers from the two tracks rarely meeting except in IEP meetings.	• Establishes collaborative models that enable specialists and regular classroom teachers to work hand in hand.

of the key differences between these two paradigms. MI theory provides a growth paradigm for assisting special-needs students in school. It acknowledges difficulties or disabilities, but does so within the context of regarding special-needs students as basically healthy individuals. MI theory suggests that "learning disabilities," for example, may occur in all seven intelligences. That is, in addition to students with dyslexia (linguistic deficit) and dyscalculia (logical-mathematical deficit), there are individuals who have prosopagnosia or specific difficulties recognizing faces (a spatial deficit), those with ideomotor dyspraxias who cannot execute specific motor commands (bodily-kinesthetic deficit), individuals who are dysmusic and have difficulty carrying a tune (musical deficit), as well as people with specific personality disorders (intrapersonal deficit) and sociopathies (interpersonal deficit). These deficits, however, often operate relatively autonomously in the midst of other dimensions of the individual's learning profile that are relatively intact and healthy. MI theory thus provides a model for understanding the autistic savant who cannot communicate clearly with others but plays music at a professional level, the dyslexic who possesses special drawing or designing gifts, the "retarded" student who can act extremely well on the stage, or the student with cerebral palsy who has special linguistic and logical-mathematical genius.

Successful Disabled Individuals as Models for Growth

It may be instructive to study the lives of eminent individuals in history who struggled with disabilities of one kind or another. Such a study reveals, in fact, the existence of people with all types of special needs who are also exceptionally gifted in one or more of the seven intelligences. Figure 11.2 lists some of these creative individuals along with the specific disability they struggled with and the primary intelligence through which they expressed much of their genius.

The persons in Figure 11.2 are known primarily for their achievements in life. In some cases, their disability was incidental to their accomplishments. In other cases, their disabilities probably helped spur them to develop their exceptional abilities. MI theory provides a context for discussing these lives and for applying the understanding gained from such study to the lives of students who are struggling with similar problems. For example, a student with dyslexia can begin to understand that his

FIGURE 11.2

High-Achieving Individuals with Disabilities

			Disability			
	LD	**CD**	**ED/BD**	**PH**	**HI**	**SI**
Linguistic Intelligence	Agatha Christie	Demosthenes	Edgar Allan Poe	Alexander Pope	Samuel Johnson	Rudyard Kipling
Logical-Mathematical Intelligence	Albert Einstein	Michael Faraday	Charles Darwin	Stephen Hawking	Thomas Edison	Johannes Kepler
Spatial Intelligence	Leonardo da Vinci	Marc Chagall	Vincent Van Gogh	Henri de Toulouse-Lautrec	Granville Redmond	Otto Litzel
Bodily-Kinesthetic Intelligence	Auguste Rodin	Admiral Peary	Vaslav Nijinsky	Jim Abbott	Marlee Matlin	Tom Sullivan
Musical Intelligence	Sergei Rachmaninoff	Maurice Ravel	Robert Schumann	Itzhak Perlman	Ludwig van Beethoven	Joaquin Rodrigo
Interpersonal Intelligence	Nelson Rockefeller	Winston Churchill	Harry Stack Sullivan	Franklin Roosevelt	King Jordan	Harry Truman
Intrapersonal Intelligence	General George Patton	Aristotle	Friedrich Nietzsche	Mohammed	Helen Keller	Aldous Huxley

LD = learning disability
CD = communicative disorder
ED/BD = emotionally disturbed/behavioral disorder

PH = physical handicap
HI = hearing impaired
SI = sight impaired

difficulty may directly affect only a small part of one intelligence area (the reading dimensions of linguistic intelligence), leaving unimpaired vast regions of his learning potential. It's instructive to note, for instance, that many great writers, including Agatha Christie and Hans Christian Andersen, have been dyslexic (see Illingworth and Illingworth 1966 and Fleming 1984).

By constructing a perspective of special-needs students as whole individuals, MI theory provides a context for envisioning positive channels through which students can learn to deal with their disabilities. Educators who view disabilities against the background of the seven intelligences see that disabilities occur in only part of a student's life; thus, they can begin to focus more attention on the *strengths* of special-needs students as a prerequisite to developing appropriate remedial strategies. Research on the "self-fulfilling prophecy" or "Pygmalion effect" suggests that the ways in which educators view a student can have a subtle but significant effect upon the quality of teaching the student receives and may help to determine the student's ultimate success or failure in school (see Rosenthal and Jacobsen 1968).

Cognitive Bypassing

Teachers and administrators need to serve as "MI strength detectives" in the lives of students facing difficulties in school. This kind of advocacy can lead the way toward providing positive solutions to their special needs. In particular, MI theory suggests that students who are not succeeding because of limitations in specific intelligence areas can often bypass these obstacles by using an alternative route, so to speak, that exploits their more highly developed intelligences (see Gardner 1983, pp. 388–392).

In some cases, special-needs students can learn to use an *alternative symbol system* in an unimpaired intelligence. The best examples of this are braille (for the seeing-impaired) and sign language (for the hearing-impaired). In each case, the linguistic symbol system (written or oral language) has been merged with bodily-kinesthetic/spatial symbol systems that require, in addition to linguistic intelligence, tactile sensitivity (for braille) and manual dexterity and physical expressiveness (for sign language). It's interesting to note that braille and sign language have both been used successfully with severely dyslexic students who possessed special strengths in spatial and kinesthetic domains (see McCoy 1975). Similarly, researchers have reported more success in teaching a group of "reading-disabled" students Chinese characters than in teaching them English sight words (Rozin, Poritsky, and Sotsky 1971). In this case, an ideographic symbol system (Chinese) worked more successfully with these spatially oriented youngsters than the linguistic (sound-symbol) English code.

In other cases, the empowering strategy will involve an *alternative technology* or special learning tool. For example, the Xerox/Kurzweil Personal Reader provides individuals who cannot decode the printed word (due to special learning or perceptual difficulties) a means of electronically scanning a printed page and having those signals transformed into sound impulses that can be heard and understood. Similarly, mathematical calculators have come to the rescue of individuals with severe dyscalculia and other math-processing difficulties. Sometimes, the empowering strategy wears a human face, as in the case of a therapist (for those struggling with difficulties in the personal intelligences), a guide (for those with physical or perceptual problems), or a tutor (for those with special learning difficulties). Figure 11.3 on page 140 lists other important empowering strategies. It shows how a difficulty in one intelligence can often be successfully overcome by rerouting a task through a more highly developed intelligence.

The same basic approach used to empower special-needs students can also be employed in developing appropriate *instructional strategies*. The underlying procedure involves translating information in the "intelligence language" that students have trouble learning or understanding into an "intelligence language" that *students do understand*. Figure 11.4 on page 141 provides a few examples.

Essentially, the approach to developing remedial strategies is the same one used in creating seven-way lesson plans and units for the regular classroom (see Chapter 5). This confluence of regular and special education methodology reinforces the fundamental growth-paradigm emphasis inherent in MI Theory. In other words, the best learning activities for special-needs students are those that are most successful with *all* students. What may be different, however, is the way in which lessons are specifically tailored to the needs of individual students or small groups of students.

FIGURE 11.3

Strategies for Bypassing Intelligence Weaknesses

	Type of Bypass Strategy						
	Linguistic	Logical-Mathematical	Spatial	Musical	Bodily-Kinesthetic	Interpersonal	Intrapersonal
Linguistic Weakness	tape recorder, Kurzweil Reader	computer languages	ideographic languages	song lyrics	braille, sign language	human readers or person to take dictation	open-ended journal
Logical-Mathematical Weakness	calculators	tutoring software programs	charts, diagrams, graphs	musical instruments as math tools	abacus and other manipulatives	math tutor	self-paced math or science programs
Spatial Weakness	talking books and tapes, talking tours	computer-assisted design (CAD)	magnifiers, maps	walking stick with tone sensor	relief maps, Mowat sensor	personal guide	self-guided tours
Bodily-Kinesthetic Weakness	"how-to" books	virtual reality	choreography diagrams	biofeedback using tones	mobility devices/motorized wheelchair	personal companion	feedback from videotape
Musical Weakness	rhythmic poetry	MIDI devices	machine that translates music into a sequence of colored lights	tapes, CDs, records	amplified vibrating musical instruments	music teacher	self-paced music lessons
Interpersonal Weakness	"talking cure" in psychotherapy	electronic bulletin boards	movies on interpersonal themes	music groups	Sierra Club/ Outward Bound	recovery/self-help support groups	individual psychotherapy
Intrapersonal Weakness	self-help books	personality self-assessment software	art therapy	music therapy	vision quest	psychotherapist	retreats, solitude

FIGURE 11.4

Examples of MI Remedial Strategies for Specific Topics

	TOPIC		
	Letter Reversals: "b" and "d"	The 3 States of Matter	Understanding Simple Fractions
Linguistic Remedial Strategy	identify through context in words or sentences	give verbal descriptions, assign reading matter	use storytelling, word problems
Logical-Mathematical Remedial Strategy	play anagrams or other word-pattern games	classify substances in the classroom	show math ratios on number line
Spatial Remedial Strategy	color code b's and d's; use stylistic features unique to each letter; create "pictures' out of letters (e.g., "bed" where the stems are the posts)	draw pictures of different states; look at pictures of molecules in different states	look at a diagram of "pies"; draw pictures
Bodily-Kinesthetic Remedial Strategy	use kinesthetic mnemonic (put fists together, thumbs upraised, palms facing you—this makes a "bed")	act out the 3 states in a dance; do hands-on lab experiments; build models of 3 states	divide apples or other food items into segments
Musical Remedial Strategy	sing songs with lots of b's and d's in them to help differentiate	play musical recording at 3 different speeds	play a fraction of a song (e.g., one note of a three-note song)
Interpersonal Remedial Strategy	give letter cards with b's and d's randomly to students; have them find others with their sound (auditorily) and then check answers visually with cards	create the 3 states as a class (each person as a molecule)	divide the class into different fraction pies
Intrapersonal Remedial Strategy	list favorite words that begin with b and d	examine the 3 states in one's body, home, and neighborhood	choose a favorite fraction and collect specific instances of it

MI Theory in the Development of IEPs

MI theory lends itself particularly well to the development of teaching strategies in individualized educational programs (IEPs) developed as part of a student's special education placement. In particular, MI theory can help teachers identify a student's strengths and preferred learning style, and this information can serve as a basis for deciding what kinds of interventions are most appropriate for inclusion in the IEP.

All too often a student having problems in a specific area will be given an IEP that neglects his most developed intelligences while concentrating on his weaknesses. For instance, let's say a student with well-developed bodily-kinesthetic and spatial intelligences is having difficulty learning to read. In many schools today, he will be given an IEP that fails to include physical and picture-oriented activities as a means of achieving his educational objectives. Frequently, the interventions suggested for such a student will include *more* linguistic tasks, such as reading programs and auditory awareness activities—in other words, more concentrated and controlled doses of the same sorts of tasks the student was failing at in the regular classroom!

MI theory suggests a fundamentally different approach: teaching through intelligences that have been previously neglected by educators working with the child. Figure 11.5 shows examples of IEPs that might be written for students who have had difficulty learning to read yet possess strengths in other intelligence areas. Note that these example accommodate the student's learning differences at both the instructional level and the assessment level.

The Broad Implications of MI Theory for Special Education

The influence that MI theory can have on special education goes far beyond the development of new remedial strategies and interventions. If MI theory is implemented on a large scale in both the regular and special education programs in a school district, it is likely to have some of the following effects:

Fewer referrals to special education classes. When the regular curriculum includes the full spectrum of intelligences, referrals to special education classes will decline. Most teachers now focus on the linguistic

FIGURE 11.5

Sample MI Plans for
Individualized Education Programs (IEPs)

Subject: Reading

Short-Term Instructional Goal: When presented with an unfamiliar piece of children's literature with a readability level of beginning 2nd grade, the student will be able to effectively decode 80 percent of the words and answer four out of five comprehension questions based on its content.

Plan 1: For a Child with Strong Bodily-Kinesthetic and Spatial Intelligences

Some Possible Materials and Strategies:

- Student can act out (mime) new words and the content of new stories.
- Student can make new words into pictures (e.g., hanging lights on the word "street").
- Student can sculpt new words using clay.
- Student can draw pictures expressing the content of books.

Assessment: Student is allowed to move his body while reading the book; student can answer content questions by drawing answers rather than (or in addition to) responding orally.

Plan 2: For a Child with Strong Musical and Interpersonal Intelligences

Some Possible Materials and Strategies:

- Student can make up songs using new words.
- Student can play board games or card games that require learning new words.
- Student can use simple song books as reading material (singing lyrics accompanied by music).
- Student can read children's literature to another child.
- Student can teach a younger child to read

Assessment: Student is allowed to sing while reading a book; student may demonstrate competency by reading a book to another child and/or answering content questions posed by a peer.

---

and mathematical intelligences, neglecting the needs of students who learn best through the musical, spatial, bodily-kinesthetic, interpersonal, or intrapersonal intelligences. It is these students who most often fail in regular classrooms and are placed in special settings. Once regular classrooms themselves become more sensitive to the needs of different kinds of learners through MI learning programs, the need for special placement, especially for learning disabilities and behavior problems, will diminish. This model thus supports the full inclusion movement in education (see Stainback, Stainback, and Forest 1989).

A Changing Role for the Special Education Teacher. The special education teacher or learning specialist will begin to function less as a "pull-out" or special class teacher and more as a special MI consultant to the regular classroom teacher. In this new role, MI consultants, perhaps operating like Gardner's student-curriculum brokers (see Chapter 9), can assist regular classroom teachers in some of the following tasks:

–Identifying students' strongest intelligences
–Focusing on the needs of specific students
–Designing MI curriculums
–Creating specific MI interventions
–Working with groups using MI activities

All or most of a special-needs/MI teacher's time can be spent in the regular classroom focusing on the individual needs of students and the targeting of special MI activities to achieve educational outcomes.

A Greater Emphasis on Identifying Strengths. Teachers assessing special-needs students will likely put more emphasis on identifying the strengths of students. Qualitative and authentic measures (such as those described in Chapters 3 and 10) are likely to have a larger role in special education and may perhaps even begin to supplant standardized diagnostic measures as a means of developing appropriate educational programs.

Increased Self-Esteem. With more emphasis placed on the strengths and abilities of special-needs children, students' self-esteem and internal locus of control are likely to rise, thus helping to promote success among a broader community of learners.

Increased Understanding and Appreciation of Students. As students use MI theory to make sense of their individual differences, their tolerance, understanding, and appreciation of those with special needs is likely to rise, making their full integration into the regular classroom more likely.

Ultimately, the adoption of MI theory (or an MI-like philosophy) in education will move special education toward a growth paradigm and facilitate a greater level of cooperation between special education and regular education. MI classrooms will then become the least restrictive environment for all special-needs students except the most disruptive.

For Further Study

1. Develop a curriculum unit for use in a regular or special-needs classroom that focuses upon famous individuals who overcame disabilities. Include biographies, videos, slides, and other materials. Discuss with students how a disability accounts for only one part of an individual's life as a total person. Use MI theory as a model for regarding disabilities as glitches in basically healthy human beings.

2. Identify a special-needs student who is currently not succeeding in the school system. Using some of the strategies suggested in Chapter 3, identify the student's strengths in terms of the theory of multiple intelligences. Brainstorm as many strengths as possible, including strengths that combine several intelligences. Then discuss with colleagues how this process of strengths assessment can affect their overall view of the student and generate new solutions for helping them.

3. Identify a special-needs student in your program who is having school-related difficulties because of limitations in one particular intelligence. Identify specific empowering tools (e.g., alternative symbol systems, learning materials, software, human resources) that can be used to help "reroute" the problem into a highly developed intelligence. Choose one or two of the most appropriate and available tools to apply to the student's particular need(s). Evaluate the results.

4. Write multiple-intelligence strategies into a student's IEP based upon the student's strengths in one or more intelligences.

5. Meet with a regular classroom teacher (if you are a special education teacher) or a specialist (if you are a regular classroom teacher) and discuss ways in which you can collaboratively use MI strategies to help special-needs kids succeed in the mainstream.

6. Work individually with a special-needs child (or a small group of children) and help him (or them) become aware of their special strengths in terms of MI theory.

12 MI and Cognitive Skills

Though man a thinking being is defined,
Few use the grand prerogative of mind.
How few think justly of the thinking few!
How many never think, who think they do!

—Jane Taylor

WITH THE ADVENT OF COGNITIVE PSYCHOLOGY as the predominant paradigm in education, educators have become increasingly interested in helping students develop thinking strategies. *How* students think has become almost more important than *what* they think about. MI theory provides an ideal context for making sense out of students' cognitive skills. The seven intelligences in the model are themselves cognitive capacities. Hence, to develop any or all of them in the ways described in previous chapters is to facilitate the cultivation of students' ability to think. It may be helpful, however, to look more specifically at how MI theory applies to the areas most often emphasized by educators espousing a cognitive approach to learning: memory, problem solving and other forms of higher order thinking, and Bloom's levels of cognitive complexity.

Memory

Classroom teachers have always seemed troubled by the problem of students' memories. "They knew it yesterday, but today it's gone" is a familiar refrain. "It's as if I never even taught it. What's the point?" many teachers lament. Helping students retain what they learn appears to be one of education's most pressing and unresolved issues. MI theory provides a helpful perspective on this age-old educational problem. It suggests that the notion of a "pure" memory is flawed. Memory, according to Howard Gardner, is intelligence-specific. There is no such thing as a "good memory" or a "bad memory" unless and until an intelligence is specified. Thus, one may have a good memory for faces (spatial/interpersonal intelligence) but a poor memory for names and dates (linguistic/logical-mathematical intelligence). One may have a superior ability to recall a tune (musical intelligence) but not be able to remember the dance step that accompanies it (bodily-kinesthetic intelligence).

This new perspective on memory suggests that students with "poor memories" may have poor memories in only one or two of the intelligences. The problem, however, may be that their poor memories are in one or both of the intelligence areas most frequently emphasized in school: linguistic and logical-mathematical intelligence. The solution, then, lies in helping these students gain access to their "good" memories in other intelligences (e.g., musical, spatial, and bodily-kinesthetic). Memory training, or work involving memorization of material in any subject, should therefore be taught in such a way that all seven "memories" are activated.

Spelling is an academic area that has typically relied heavily upon memory skills. Unfortunately, most instructional approaches to studying spelling words have involved the use of only linguistic strategies: write the word five times, use the word in a sentence, spell the word out loud, and so forth. MI theory suggests that problem spellers may need to go beyond these auditory, oral, and written strategies (all linguistic) to find success. Here are some examples of how the orthographic structure of linguistic symbols (i.e., the English alphabet) can be linked to other intelligences to enhance the retention of spelling words:

Musical Intelligence: Spelling words can be sung. For example, any seven-letter word (or multiple of seven) can be sung to the tune of "Twinkle, Twinkle Little Star," and any six-letter word can be sung to the tune of "Happy Birthday to You."

Spatial Intelligence: Spelling words can be visualized. Students can be introduced to an "inner blackboard" or other mental screen in their mind's eye. During study, students place words on the mental screen; during test time, students simply refer to their "inner blackboard" for help.

Other spatial approaches include: color coding spelling patterns; drawing spelling words as pictures (e.g., the word "sun" can be drawn with rays of light emanating from the word); reducing spelling words to "configurations" or graphic outlines showing spatial placement of stems.

Logical-Mathematical Intelligence: Spelling words can be "digitalized," that is, reduced to a series of 0s and 1s (consonants = 1; vowels = 0); spelling words can also be coded using other sorts of number systems (e.g., assigning a number to a letter depending upon its placement in the alphabet: a = 1, b = 2, etc.).

Bodily-Kinesthetic Intelligence: Spelling words can be translated into sign language or whole-body movements. Other bodily-kinesthetic approaches include tracing spelling words in sand, molding spelling words in clay, and using body movements to show patterns in words (e.g., stand up on the vowels, sit down on the consonants).

Interpersonal Intelligence: Words can be spelled by a group of people. For example, each student has a letter and, when a word is called, students who have the letters in the word form the word with the other students.

Intrapersonal Intelligence: Students spell words developmentally (i.e., the way they think they're spelled) or students learn to spell words that have an emotional charge (organic spelling).

The task for you as a teacher, then, is to help students associate the material to be learned with components of the different intelligences: words, numbers, pictures, physical movements, musical phrases, social interactions, and personal feelings and experiences. After students have been exposed to memory strategies from all seven intelligences, they will be able to pick out those strategies that work best for them, and be able to use them independently during personal study periods.

Problem Solving

Although research studies suggest that over the past few years American students have improved their performance on rote learning tasks such as spelling and arithmetic, they place American students far down the achievement ladder in comparisons with other countries on measures of higher order cognitive processes (Fiske 1987, 1988). In particular, U.S. students' problem-solving abilities have been regarded as in need of significant improvement. Consequently, more and more educators are looking for ways to help students *think* more effectively when confronted with academic problems. Unfortunately, the bias in the recent critical-thinking movement has been in the direction of logical-mathematical reasoning abilities and in the use of self-talk or other linguistic strategies. MI theory suggests that *thinking* can and frequently does go far beyond these two areas. To illustrate what these other forms of problem-solving behavior "look" like, it may be helpful to review the thinking processes of eminent individuals whose discoveries have helped shape the world we live in (see John-Steiner 1987, Gardner 1993b). By studying the "end-states" of specific problem-solving processes in these great people, educators can learn much that can help foster the same sort of processes in their students.

Many thinkers have used imagery and picture language (*spatial* intelligence) to help them in their work. A study of Charles Darwin's notebooks reveals that he used the image of a tree to help him generate the theory of evolution: "Organized beings represent a tree, irregularly branched, . . . as many terminal buds dying as new ones generated" (Gruber 1977, p. 126). The physicist John Howarth was more explicit in describing his problem-solving processes:

> I make abstract pictures. I just realized that the process of abstraction in the pictures in my head is similar to the abstraction you engage in dealing with physical problems analytically. You reduce the number of variables, simplify and consider what you hope is the essential part of the situation you are dealing with; then you apply your analytical techniques. In making a visual picture it is possible to choose one which contains representations of only the essential elements— a simplified picture, abstracted from a number of other pictures and containing their common elements (John-Steiner 1987, pp. 84–85).

Others have used problem-solving strategies that combine visual-spatial images with certain kinetic or *bodily-kinesthetic* features of the mind. For example, Albert Einstein frequently performed "thought-experiments" that helped him develop his relativity theory, including a fantasy that involved riding on the end of a beam of light. When asked by a French mathematician to describe his thinking processes, Einstein said they included elements that were of *visual* and *muscular* type (see Ghiselin 1955, p. 43). Similarly, Henri Poincaré shares the story of how he struggled for days with a vexing mathematical problem:

> For fifteen days I strove to prove that there could not be any functions like those I have since called Fuchsian functions. I was then very

ignorant; every day I seated myself at my work table, stayed an hour or two, tried a great number of combinations and reached no results. One evening, contrary to my custom, I drank black coffee and could not sleep. Ideas rose in crowds; *I felt them collide until pairs interlocked* [italics mine], so to speak, making a stable combination. By the next morning, I had established the existence of a class of Fuchsian functions, those which come from the hypergeometric series; I had only to write out the results which took but a few hours (Ghiselin 1955, p. 36).

Musicians speak about a very different kind of problem-solving capacity, one that involves access to musical imagery. Mozart explained his own composing process this way: "Nor do I hear in my imagination the parts [of the composition] successively, but I hear them, as it were, all at once. What a delight this is I cannot tell. All this inventing, this producing, takes place in a pleasing lively dream" (Ghiselin 1955, p. 45). Einstein acknowledged the operation of musical thought in a logical-mathematical/spatial domain when, referring to Nils Bohr's model of the atom with its orbiting electrons absorbing and releasing energy, he wrote, "this is the highest form of musicality in the sphere of thought" (Clark 1972, p. 292).

There are even processes unique to the personal intelligences. For example, a commentator reflecting on the interpersonal intelligence of Lyndon B. Johnson said, "Lots of guys can be smiling and deferential. He had something else. No matter what someone thought, Lyndon would agree with him—would be there ahead of him, in fact. He could follow someone's mind around—and figure out where it was going and beat it there" (Caro 1990). In a more intrapersonal fashion, Marcel Proust used simple sensations like the taste of a pastry to evoke inner feelings that swept him back into the days of his childhood—a context that provided the basis for his masterwork, *Remembrance of Things Past* (see Proust 1928, pp. 54–58).

How these "end-state" cognitive processes translate into classroom practice may seem at first elusive. It is possible, however, to distill certain basic elements from the problem-solving strategies of the geniuses of culture and create strategies that can be learned even by students in the primary grades. For example, students can learn to "visualize" their ideas in much the same way Einstein performed his thought-experiments. They can learn to sketch metaphorical images that relate to problems they are working on much as Darwin worked with images in his own notebooks. The following list indicates the wide range of MI problem-solving strategies that could be used by students in academic settings:

Linguistic Intelligence: Self-talk or thinking out loud (see Perkins 1981).

Logical-Mathematical Intelligence: Logical heuristics (see Polya 1957).

Spatial Intelligence: Visualization, idea sketching, mind-mapping (see McKim 1980 and Margulies 1991).

Bodily-Kinesthetic Intelligence: Kinesthetic imagery (see Gordon and Poze 1966); also, accessing "gut feelings" or using one's hands, fingers, or whole body to solve problems.

Musical Intelligence: Sensing the "rhythm" or "melody" of a problem (e.g., harmony vs. dissonance); using music to unlock problem-solving capacities (see Ostrander and Schroeder 1979).

Interpersonal Intelligence: Bouncing ideas off other people (see Johnson, Johnson, Roy, and Holubec 1984).

Intrapersonal Intelligence: Identifying with the problem; accessing dream imagery, personal feelings that relate to the problem; deep introspection (see Harman and Rheingold 1984).

Once students have been introduced to strategies like these, they can choose from a cognitive menu the approaches that are likely to be successful for them in any given learning situation. This kind of cognitive training can prove far richer than the traditional "thinking skills" program, which all too often consists of worksheets containing games and puzzles or overhead sheets detailing the five-step sequence involved in solving a math word problem. In the future, when students are urged by a teacher to "think harder," students will have the luxury of asking, "In which intelligence?"

Promoting Chistopherian Encounters

In his book *The Unschooled Mind,* Howard Gardner (1991) addresses the tendency of contemporary schooling to teach students surface-level knowledge without ever affecting their deeper understanding of the world. As a result, students are graduating from high school, college, and even graduate school still holding on to many of the same naive beliefs they held as preschoolers. In one example, 70 percent of college students who had completed a physics course in mechanics said that a coin tossed up in the air has two forces acting upon it, the downward force of gravity and the upward force coming from the hand (the truth is only gravity exerts a force) (Gardner 1991, p. 154). Supposedly well-educated students, who can spout algorithms, rules, laws, and principles in a variety of domains, still harbor, according to Gardner, a mine field of misconceptions, rigidly applied procedures, stereotypes, and simplifications, What is required is an approach to education that challenges naive beliefs, provokes questions, invites multiple perspectives, and ultimately stretches a student's mind to the point where it can apply existing knowledge to new situations and novel contexts.

Gardner suggests that a student's mind can be expanded through the use of "Christopherian encounters." Although Gardner uses the term specifically in reference to exploding misconceptions in the field of science, this phrases can serve as a beautiful metaphor for the expansion in general of a child's multiple intelligences to higher levels of competence and understanding. Just as Christopher Columbus challenged the notion that the earth is flat by sailing "beyond the edge" and thereby showing its curved shape, so, too, Gardner suggests that educators challenge students' limited beliefs by taking them "over the edge" into areas where they must confront the contradictions and disjunctions in their own thinking. It's possible to apply this general approach to multiple intelligences theory by suggesting examples in which students' minds might be stretched in each of the intelligences:

Linguistic Intelligence: Moving students beyond the literal interpretation of a piece of literature (e.g., the novel *Moby Dick* is more than a sea yarn about a whale).

Logical-Mathematical Intelligence: Devising science experiments that force students to confront contradictions in their thinking about natural phenomena (e.g., asking students to predict how a ball rolled straight from the center of a rotating merry-go-round will move as it reaches the edge and then discussing the outcome).

Spatial Intelligence: Helping students confront tacit beliefs about art that might, for example, include the prejudice that paintings should use pleasant colors and depict beautiful scenery and attractive people (e.g., showing students Picasso's painting *Guernica*, which does not contain those characteristics).

Bodily-Kinesthetic Intelligence: Moving students beyond stereotypical ways of using their bodies to express certain feelings or ideas in a dance or play (e.g., helping students explore the wide range of body postures and facial expressions for expressing Willy Loman's sense of defeat in Arthur Miller's *Death of a Salesman.*

Musical Intelligence: Assisting students in undoing stereotypes that might suggest that good music should be harmonious and have a regular beat (e.g., playing students Stravinsky's *Rite of Spring*—a piece that caused a riot when first played because it clashed with the listeners' beliefs about what was good music).

Interpersonal Intelligence: Helping students go beyond the imputation of simplistic motivations in studying fictional or real characters in literature, history, or other fields (e.g., helping students understand that Holden Caulfield's impetus in *Catcher in the Rye* involved more than a desire for a "night on the town," or that Adolf Hitler's rise to power was motivated by more than a "thirst for power").

Intrapersonal Intelligence: Deepening students' understanding of themselves by relating different parts of the curriculum to their own personal life experiences and backgrounds (e.g., asking students to think of the "Huck Finn" or "Laura Ingalls Wilder" part of themselves).

Multiple-intelligence theory must be seen as more than simply a process by which students celebrate and begin to activate their many ways of knowing. Educators must assist students in developing higher levels of understanding through their multiple intelligences. By making certain that "Christopherian encounters" are a regular part of the school day—in each intelligence—educators can help ensure that the unschooled mind will truly develop into a powerful and creative thinking force.

MI Theory and Bloom's Levels of Cognitive Complexity

Almost forty years ago, University of Chicago professor Benjamin S. Bloom (1956) unveiled his famous "taxonomy of educational objectives."

This survey included a cognitive domain, and its six levels of complexity have been used over the past four decades as a gauge by which educators can ensure that instruction stimulates and develops students' higher order thinking capacities. The six levels are:

• *Knowledge:* Rote memory skills (knowing facts, terms, procedures, classification systems).
• *Comprehension:* The ability to translate, paraphrase, interpret, or extrapolate material.
• *Application:* The capacity to transfer knowledge from one setting to another.
• *Analysis:* Discovering and differentiating the component parts of a larger whole.
• *Synthesis:* Weaving together component parts into a coherent whole.
• *Evaluation:* Judging the value or utility of information using a set of standards.

Bloom's taxonomy provides a kind of quality-control mechanism through which you can judge how deeply students' minds have been stirred by a multiple-intelligence curriculum. It would be easy to construct MI instructional methods that appeared compelling—owing to the wide range of intelligences addressed—but that kept learning at the knowledge or rote level of cognitive complexity. MI activities for teaching spelling, the times tables, or history facts are prime examples of MI theory in the service of lower order cognitive skills. MI curriculums, however, can be designed to incorporate all of Bloom's levels of cognitive complexity. The curriculum outline presented in Figure 12.1 shows how a teacher can articulate competencies that address all seven intelligences as well Bloom's six levels of cognitive complexity.

You don't have to include all of these tasks in one unit. In fact, you may at first want to develop a thematic curriculum without reference to MI theory and Bloom's taxonomy. You can simply use the instructional model displayed in Figure 12.1 as a road map to help you stay on course in your efforts to address a number of intelligences and cognitive levels. It may become apparent, for example, after laying the MI/Bloom template over the curriculum, that some easily incorporated musical experiences are missing from the unit, or that there are no opportunities for students to evaluate experiences—something that can be easily remedied. MI theory represents a model that can enable you to move beyond heavily linguistic,

155

FIGURE 12.1

MI Theory and Bloom's Taxonomy

Ecology Unit: Local environment—trees in your neighborhood

	Knowledge	Comprehension	Application	Analysis	Synthesis	Evaluation
				Bloom's Six Levels of Educational Objectives		
Linguistic Intelligence	memorize names of trees	explain how trees receive nutrients	given description of tree diseases, suggest cause of each disease	list parts of tree	explain how a tree functions in relation to the ecosystem	rate different methods of controlling tree growth
Logical-Mathematical Intelligence	remember number of points on specific trees' leaves	convert English to metric in calculating height of tree	given height of smaller tree, estimate height of larger tree	analyze materials found in sap residue	given weather, soil, and other information, chart projected growth of a tree	rate different kinds of tree nutrients based on data
Spatial Intelligence	remember basic configurations of specific trees	look at diagrams of trees and tell what stage of growth they are in	use geometric principles to determine height of tree	draw cellular structure of tree root	create a landscaping plan using trees as central feature	evaluate practicality of different landscaping plans
Bodily-Kinesthetic Intelligence	identify tree by the feel of the bark	given array of tree fruits, identify seeds	given type of local tree, find an ideal location for planting it	create different parts of tree from clay	gather all materials needed for planting a tree	evaluate the quality of different kinds of fruit
Musical Intelligence	remember songs that deal with trees	explian how old tree songs came into being	change the lyrics of an old tree song to reflect current issues	classify songs by issue and historical period	create your own tree song based on information in this unit	rate the songs from best to worst and give reasons for your choices
Interpersonal Intelligence	record responses to the question "What is your favorite tree?"	determine the most popular tree in class by interviewing others	use survey results to pick location for field trip to orchard	classify kids into groups according to favorite tree	arrange field trip to orchard by contacting necessary people	rank three methods to ask others about tree preference
Intrapersonal Intelligence	remember a time you climbed a tree	share the primary feeling you had while up in the tree	develop "tree-climbing rules" based upon your experience	divide up your experience into "beginning," "middle," and "end"	plan a tree-climbing expedition based on your past experience	explain what you liked "best" and "least" about your experience

lower order thinking activities (e.g., worksheets) into a broad range of complex cognitive tasks that prepare students for life.

For Further Study

1. Write ten to fifteen random words on the board (words that are at students' level of decoding and comprehension). Give the class one minute to "memorize" them. Then cover the words and ask students to write all the words from memory (in any order). Provide immediate feedback. Discuss the strategies that students used to remember the words. Then teach them memory strategies using several intelligences:

• *Linguistic:* String the words together in some kind of intelligible story.
• *Spatial:* Visualize the story taking place.
• *Musical:* Sing the story to a set tune or a tune composed on the spot.
• *Bodily-Kinesthetic/Interpersonal:* Act out the story, emphasizing the body movements involved for each of the words.
• *Intrapersonal:* Associate personal experiences (and accompanying feelings) with each word.

Practice these strategies using another list of words, and then have students write the list from memory. Discuss what was different this time (have students talk about which strategies seemed most successful to them). After using this procedure with two or three more lists, have students use these memory strategies for curriculum-related material (e.g., history facts, spelling words, vocabulary, etc.).

2. Have students solve a brainteaser or other logical-mathematical problem involving higher order thinking processes. Allow students ten to fifteen minutes to use whatever strategies they wish. Let them know they can work with other people, walk around, ask for resources, and so on. Then have students share their particular strategies or problem-solving processes, writing them on the board as they are given. After everyone has had a chance to share, go over the list of strategies and note which intelligences have been tapped. Ask students: Are some strategies more successful than others? Are certain strategies or problem-solving processes more *fun* than others?

Using other types of problems, repeat this activity. Keep a list of problem-solving strategies organized by primary intelligence. Display the list so students can refer to it throughout the year as a resource in guiding their own study habits.

3. Develop a thematic unit, or take a unit that you've already developed, and note which intelligences and levels of cognitive complexity are developed through the activities in the unit. List additional activities that might enhance the intellectual breadth and cognitive depth of the unit.

4. Create "Christopherian encounters" for materials in your curriculum that will stretch students' minds, challenge existing beliefs, and bring students' multiple intelligences to higher levels of functioning.

13 Other Applications of MI Theory

> At present, the notion of schools devoted to multiple intelligences is still in its infancy, and there are as many plausible recipes as there are educational chefs. I hope that in the next twenty years, a number of efforts will be made to craft an education that takes multiple intelligences seriously; should this be done, we will be in a position to know which of these "thought" and "action experiments" make sense and which prove to be impractical or ill-advised.
>
> —Howard Gardner (1993, p. 250)

IN ADDITION TO THE AREAS COVERED IN previous chapters, there are many other potential applications of MI theory to education. Three that deserve mention before ending this book include computer technology, cultural diversity, and career counseling. In each case, MI theory provides a context through which existing understandings and resources can be extended to include a broader perspective. This wider view, in turn, can allow educators to develop educational materials and strategies that meet the needs of a more diverse student population.

Computer Technology

Our first inclination may be to associate computers with logical-mathematical intelligence. This connection arises in large part because of the stereotypical images of "computer nerds" working on spreadsheets or toiling over highly abstract computer programming languages. Computers themselves, however, are intelligence-neutral mechanisms. What activates computers are the software programs used to run them. And these software programs can be designed to interface with any or all of the seven intelligences. Word processing software, for example, calls forth from its users a certain level of linguistic intelligence. Draw-and-paint software, on the other hand, more often requires spatial intelligence. The list of program types in Figure 13.1 on page 160 suggests the broad range of software available to activate the multiple intelligences; examples of specific products are provided in parentheses.

You can use MI theory as a basis for selecting and making available software for use in the classroom or in specially designated computer labs in the school. Perhaps the most exciting technology application involving multiple intelligences is emerging in the area of hypertext. Through multiple stacking of "cards" in a program stored on a CD-ROM disc, a project incorporating word text (linguistic), illustrations (spatial), sound score (musical or linguistic), and video data (bodily-kinesthetic and other intelligences) can be developed. For example, a student could create a learning project on horticulture. The computer program might begin with a written text describing local flowers (linguistic) accompanied by statistical charts listing the planting requirements of specific flowers (logical-mathematical). By clicking the electronic mouse on specific nouns in the text—the word "rose" perhaps—an illustration of a rose might appear (spatial) along with a song mentioning the rose—for instance, "The Rose" sung by Bette Midler (musical). Clicking on specific verbs—for example, "to plant"—might activate a video presentation of the student planting a flower (bodily-kinesthetic).

The act of putting together such a multimedia project requires a great deal of intrapersonal intelligence. And if such a project is cooperative in nature (a class gardening project perhaps), then interpersonal intelligence is called into play as well. The completed CD-ROM discs themselves become valuable documents of a student's learning progress. They can serve as "electronic portfolios" that can easily be passed from one teacher to the next as part of an authentic assessment of the student's accomplishments during the year (CD technology specifically designed to facilitate such assessment purposes is already available; see, for example, The Grady Profile available from Aurbach and Associates, Inc., 8233 Tulane Ave., St. Louis, MO 63132; see also Campbell 1992).

Cultural Diversity

Over the past two decades, American education has seen tremendous demographic changes that have created a student population more racially,

FIGURE 13.1
Software That Activates the Multiple Intelligences

Linguistic Intelligence
- word processing programs (WordPerfect)
- typing tutors (Mavis Beacon Teaches Typing!)
- desktop publishing programs (Publish It!)
- electronic libraries (World Library)
- interactive storybooks (Just Grandma and Me)
- word games (Missing Links)

Logical-Mathematical Intelligence
- math skills tutorials (Math Blaster)
- computer programming tutors (LOGO)
- logic games (King's Rule)
- science programs (Science Tool Kits)
- critical thinking programs (HOTS—Higher Order Thinking Skills)

Spatial Intelligence
- animation programs (Art and Film Director)
- draw-and-paint programs (Dazzle Draw)
- electronic chess games (Chessmaster)
- spatial problem-solving games (Tetris)
- electronic puzzle kits (Living Jigsaws)
- clip-art programs (The New Print Shop)
- geometry programs (Sensei's Geometry)
- graphic presentations of knowledge (World GeoGraph)

Bodily-Kinesthetic Intelligence
- hands-on construction kits that interface with computers (LEGO to LOGO)
- motion-simulation games (Flight Simulator)
- virtual-reality system software (Dactyl Nightmare)
- eye-hand coordination games (Shufflepuck Cafe)
- tools that plug into computers (Science Toolkit)

Musical Intelligence
- music literature tutors (Exploratorium)
- singing software [transforms voice input into synthesizer sounds] (Vocalizer)
- composition software (Music Studio)
- tone recognition and melody memory enhancers (Arnold)
- musical instrument digital interfaces—i.e., MIDI (Music Quest MIDI Starter System)

Interpersonal Intelligence
- electronic bulletin boards (Kidsnet)
- simulation games (Sim City)

Intrapersonal Intelligence
- personal choice software (Decisions, Decisions)
- career counseling software (The Perfect Career)
- any self-paced program (e.g., most of the above programs)

ethnically, and culturally diverse than ever before. Such diversity presents a great challenge for educators in designing curriculums that are not only *content*-sensitive to cultural differences (e.g., exposing students to the beliefs, background, and foundations of individual cultures), but also *process*-sensitive (e.g., helping students understand the many "ways of knowing" that different cultures possess). MI theory provides a model that is culturally sensitive to such differences. As such, it provides educators with a valuable tool to help celebrate the ways in which different cultures think.

According to MI theory, an intelligence must be valued by a culture in order to be considered a true intelligence. This criteria automatically disqualifies many of the tasks that have traditionally been associated with intelligence testing in the schools. For example, the ability to repeat random digits backward and forward is a task found on some intelligence tests, even though this feat is not particularly valued by any culture. Nowhere in the world do a culture's elders pass on random digits to the next generation. What cultures do pass on to their younger members are stories, myths, great art and music, scientific discoveries, social mores, political institutions, and number systems—among many other "end-states" of accomplishment.

All cultures in the world possess and make use of the seven intelligences in MI theory; however, the ways in which they do so, and the manner in which individual intelligences are valued, vary considerably. A person growing up among the Puluwat culture in the South Sea Islands, for example, would discover that spatial intelligence is highly prized because of its use in navigating the seas (see Gladwin 1970). Puluwat peoples live on several hundred islands, and the ability to move easily from one island to another has a high cultural value. They train their children from a very early age to recognize the constellations, the various "bumps" (islands) on the horizon, and the different textures on the surface of the water that point to significant geographical information. The chief navigators in that society have more prestige than even the political leaders.

In some cultures, musical intelligence is a capacity that is considered universal among all members rather than the province of an elite group of performers. Children growing up among the Anang in Nigeria are expected to learn hundreds of dances and songs by the time they are five years old. In Hungary, because of the pioneering influence of the composer Zoltán Kodály on education, students are exposed to music everyday and are expected to learn to read musical notation. There are also cultures that place a greater emphasis upon connectedness between peoples (interpersonal intelligence) than upon the individual going his own way (intrapersonal intelligence) (see Gardner 1983).

It's important to repeat, however, that every culture has and uses all seven intelligences. Educators would be making a great mistake if they began to refer to specific racial or ethnic groups only in terms of one intelligence. The history of intelligence testing is filled with such bigotry and narrow-mindedness (see, for example, Gould 1981). Indiscriminate use of MI theory in discussions of cultural differences might well revive old racist stereotypes (e.g., "blacks are musical" and "Asians are logical"). For a list of some of the ways in which cultural groups value each of the seven intelligences, see Figure 1.1, "Ways That Cultures Value" (p. 7).

Such a broad perspective on culture can provide a context for exploring in a school setting the tremendous diversity in the ways different cultures express themselves through each of the seven intelligences. You might want to periodically hold multicultural/multiple-intelligence fairs in your school to celebrate such differences. You could could develop curriculums that integrate MI theory into multicultural units. And you can also introduce students to MI theory through great figures in each culture who have achieved high "end-state" performances in each of the seven intelligences (see Figure 13.2 for some examples).

Career Counseling

Because it emphasizes the broad range of ways in which adults pursue their work in life, MI theory provides an appropriate vehicle for helping youngsters begin to develop vocational aspirations. If students are exposed from a very early age to a wide variety of adults demonstrating real-life skills in all seven intelligences, they will have a firm basis upon which to launch a career once they leave school. In the early grades, students would benefit by having adults come into class to talk about their life's work, and by going to visit adults at their places of work. It is important that educators *not* attempt to match children's proclivities to specific careers too early in their development. By seeing the spectrum of occupations related to each of the seven intelligences through these kinds of visits and field trips, children can begin making their own decisions about what feels right and what doesn't fit vocationally. Children also benefit

FIGURE 13.2
Eminent Individuals from Minority Cultures

	African American	Asian American	Latino American	Native American
High Linguistic Intelligence	Toni Morrison	Amy Tan	Isabel Allende	Vine de Loria
High Logical-Mathematical Intelligence	George Washington Carver	Yuan Lee	Luis Alvarez	Robert Whitman
High Spatial Intelligence	Spike Lee	I. M. Pei	Frida Kahlo	Oscar Howe
High Bodily-Kinesthetic Intelligence	Jackie Joyner-Kersee	Kristi Yamaguchi	Juan Marichal	Jim Thorpe
High Musical Intelligence	Scott Joplin	Midori	Linda Ronstadt	Buffy Sainte Marie
High Interpersonal Intelligence	Martin Luther King, Jr.	Daniel K. Inouye	Xavier L. Suarez	Russell Means
High Intrapersonal Intelligence	Malcolm X	S. I. Hayakawa	Caesar Chavez	Black Elk

from periodic discussions about "what they'd like to be when they grow up." Plan on using the MI vocabulary in these discussions to help frame some of their aspirations.

At the middle and secondary school levels, students can participate in an ongoing process of self-assessment to determine what they are temperamentally and cognitively suited for in the job marketplace (the MI self-assessment tools may be useful in the process). Here is a list of occupations categorized by primary intelligence:

• **Linguistic Intelligence:** librarian, archivist, curator, speech pathologist, writer, radio or TV announcer, journalist, legal assistant, lawyer, secretary, typist, proofreader, English teacher

• **Logical-Mathematical Intelligence:** auditor, accountant, purchasing agent, underwriter, mathematician, scientist, statistician, actuary, computer analyst, economist, technician, bookkeeper, science teacher

• **Spatial Intelligence:** engineer, surveyor, architect, urban planner, graphic artist, interior decorator, photographer, art teacher, inventor, cartographer, pilot, fine artist, sculptor

• **Bodily-Kinesthetic Intelligence:** physical therapist, recreational worker, dancer, actor, farmer, mechanic, carpenter, craftsperson, physical education teacher, factory worker, choreographer, professional athlete, forest ranger, jeweler

• **Musical Intelligence:** disc jockey, musician, instrument maker, piano tuner, music therapist, instrument salesperson, songwriter, studio engineer, choral director, conductor, singer, music teacher, musical copyist

• **Interpersonal Intelligence:** administrator, manager, school principal, personnel worker, arbitrator, sociologist, anthropologist, counselor, psychologist, nurse, public relations person, salesperson, travel agent, social director

• **Intrapersonal Intelligence:** psychologist, clergyman, psychology teacher, therapist, counselor, theologian, program planner, entrepreneur

Of course, virtually every job consists of a variety of responsibilities touching on several intelligences. For example, school administrators must possess interpersonal intelligence to facilitate their work with teachers, parents, students, and the community. But they must also have logical-mathematical capabilities to plan budgets and schedules, and linguistic skills to write proposals and grants or to communicate effectively with others. They must also have good intrapersonal intelligence if they are to have enough confidence in themselves to stick by their decisions. When discussing careers with secondary students, it may be helpful to discuss the multiplicity of intelligences required for each job.

For Further Study

1. Assess your classroom or school's software collection. Note which specific intelligences are activated through each program. Identify intelligence areas that appear to have few or no software programs represented. Obtain catalogs of major educational software companies and list software programs that could be purchased to expand the range of intelligences covered in your school. Provide your classroom or lab with at least one

software program for each intelligence. Then label software programs by intelligences developed, and encourage students to explore a range of programs during special "choice" times.

2. Develop expertise in the use of hypertext and multimedia software. Then use these resources to help students develop special projects or "electronic portfolios" for assessment purposes.

3. Create a multicultural/multiple-intelligence unit for your class. If your community is diverse, focus on cultures represented by students in your classroom or school. In the unit, explore how different cultures express themselves through the seven intelligences, examining oral and written traditions, number systems or sciences, music, art, dance, sports, political and social systems, and religious and mythic traditions.

4. Develop a vocational curriculum unit appropriate for your classroom (planning field trips and parent visits at the elementary level, self-assessments and specific study of careers at the middle school and high school levels).

5. What are some educational applications of MI theory that have not been mentioned in this book? How might these applications best be developed? Select one unexplored area that has particular interest for you and design a unique expression of it in your classroom or school.

References

Armstrong, M. (1980). *Closely Observed Children*. London: Writers and Readers.

Armstrong, T. (1987a). "Describing Strengths in Children Identified as 'Learning Disabled' Using Howard Gardner's Theory of Multiple Intelligences as an Organizing Framework." *Dissertation Abstracts International* 48, 08A. (University Microfilms No, 87-25, 844)

Armstrong, T. (1987b). *In Their Own Way: Discovering and Encouraging Your Child's Personal Learning Style*. New York: Tarcher/Putnam.

Armstrong, T. (1988). "Learning Differences—Not Disabilities." *Principal* 68, 1: 34–36.

Armstrong, T. (1993). *7 Kinds of Smart*. New York: Plume/Penguin.

Bloom, B. (1956). *Taxonomy of Educational Objectives*. New York: David McKay.

Bonny, H., and L. Savary (1990). *Music and Your Mind*. Barrytown, N.Y.: Station Hill Press.

Campbell, J. (May 1992). "Laser Disk Portfolios: Total Child Assessment." *Educational Leadership* 49, 8: 69–70.

Carini, P. (1977). *The Art of Seeing and the Visibility of the Person*. Grand Forks, N.D.: North Dakota Study Group on Evaluation (Center for Teaching and Learning, University of North Dakota, Grand Forks, N.D. 58202).

Caro, R. (1990). *Means of Ascent*. New York: Knopf.

Clark, R. W. (1972). *Einstein: The Life and Times*. New York: Avon.

Cohen, D. L. (June 5, 1991). " 'Flow Room,' Testing Psychologist's Concept, Introduces 'Learning in Disguise,' at Key School." *Education Week*, pp. 6–7.

Csikszentmihalyi, M. (1990). *Flow: The Psychology of Optimal Experience*. New York: Harper & Row.

Dreikurs, R., and V. Soltz. (1964). *Children: The Challenge*. New York: Hawthorn.

Edwards, B. (1979). *Drawing on the Right Side of the Brain*. Los Angeles: Jeremy P. Tarcher.

Engel, B. S. (1979). *Informal Evaluation*. Grank Forks, N.D.: North Dakota Study Group on Evaluation (Center for Teaching and Learning, University of North Dakota, Grand Forks, N.D. 58202).

Feldman, D. H. (1980). *Beyond Universals in Cognitive Development*. Norwood, N.J.: Ablex.

Fiske, E. B. (January 11, 1987). "U.S. Pupils Lag in Math Ability, 3 Studies Find." *The New York Times*, pp. A1, A17–A18.

Fiske, E. B. (May 24, 1988). "In Indiana, Public School Makes 'Frills' Standard." *The New York Times*, pp. A16–A17.

Fiske, E. B. (June 8, 1988). "Schools' 'Back-to-Basics' Drive Found to Be Working in Math." *The New York Times,* pp. A1, A28.

Fleming, E. (1984). *Believe the Heart: Our Dyslexic Days.* San Francisco, Calif.: Strawberry Hill Press.

Gardner, H. (March 1979). "The Child Is Father to the Metaphor." *Psychology Today* 12, 10: 81–91.

Gardner, H. (1983). *Frames of Mind: The Theory of Multiple Intelligences.* New York: Basic Books.

Gardner, H. (May 1987). "Beyond IQ: Education and Human Development." *Harvard Educational Review* 57, 2: 187–193.

Gardner, H. (1991) *The Unschooled Mind.* New York: Basic Books.

Gardner, H. (1993a). *Multiple Intelligences: The Theory in Practice.* New York: Basic Books.

Gardner, H. (1993b). *Creating Minds.* New York: Basic Books.

Gentile, J. R. (1988). *Instructional Improvement: Summary and Analysis of Madeline Hunter's Essential Elements of Instruction and Supervision.* Oxford, Ohio: National Staff Development Council.

Ghiselin, B. (1955). *The Creative Process.* New York: Mentor.

Gladwin, T. (1970). *East Is a Big Bird: Navigation and Logic on Puluwat Atoll.* Cambridge, Mass.: Harvard University Press.

Goodlad, J. I. (1984). *A Place Called School: Prospects for the Future.* New York: McGraw-Hill.

Goodman, J., and M. Weinstein. (1980). *Playfair: Everybody's Guide to Noncompetitive Play.* San Luis Obispo, Calif.: Impact.

Gordon, W. J. J., and T. Poze. (1966). *The Metaphorical Way of Learning and Knowing.* Cambridge, Mass.: Porpoise.

Gould, S. J. (1981). *The Mismeasure of Man.* New York: W. W. Norton.

Gruber, H. (1977). "Darwin's 'Tree of Nature' and Other Images of Wide Scope," in *On Aesthetics in Science,* edited by J. Wechsler. Cambridge, Mass.: MIT Press.

Hart, L. (March 1981). "Don't Teach Them; Help Them Learn." *Learning* 9, 8: 39–40.

Harman, W., and H. Rheingold. (1984). *Higher Creativity: Liberating the Unconscious for Breakthrough Insights.* Los Angeles: Jeremy P. Tarcher.

Herman, J. L., P. R. Aschbacher, and L. Winters. (1992). *A Practical Guide to Alternative Assessment.* Alexandria, Va.: ASCD.

Holden, C. (June 8, 1979). "Paul MacLean and the Triune Brain." *Science* 204: 1068.

Illingworth, R. S., and C. M. Illingworth. (1966). *Lessons from Childhood: Some Aspects of the Early Life of Unusual Men and Women.* London: Livingstone.

Johnson, D., R. Johnson, P. Roy, and E. Holubec (1984). *Circles of Learning: Cooperation in the Classroom.* Alexandria, Va.: ASCD.

John-Steiner, V. (1987). *Notebooks of the Mind: Explorations of Thinking.* New York: Harper and Row.

Kovalik, S. (1993). *ITI: The Model—Integrated Thematic Instruction.* 2nd ed. Village of Oak Creek, Ariz.: Books for Educators.

McCoy, L. E. (1975). "Braille: A Language for Severe Dyslexics." *Journal of Learning Disabilities* 8, 5: 34.

McKim, R. H. (1980). *Experiences in Visual Thinking.* 2nd ed. Boston: PWS Engineering.

Marzano, R. J., R. S. Brandt, C. S. Hughes, B. F. Jones, B. Z. Presseisen, and S. C. Rankin. (1988). *Dimensions of Thinking: A Framework for Curriculum and Instruction.* Alexandria, Va.: ASCD.

Margulies, N. (1991). *Mapping Inner Space: Learning and Teaching Mind Mapping.* Tucson, Ariz.: Zephyr Press.

Miller, A. (1981). *The Drama of the Gifted Child.* New York: Basic Books.

Montessori, M. (1972). *The Secret of Childhood.* New York: Ballantine.

Olson, L. (January 27, 1988). "Children 'Flourish' Here: 8 Teachers and a Theory Changed a School World." *Education Week* VII, 18: 1, 18–19.

Ostrander, S., and L. Schroeder. (1979). *Superlearning.* New York: Delta.

Paul, R. (1992). *Critical Thinking: What Every Person Needs to Survive in a Rapidly Changing World.* Santa Rosa, Calif.: Foundation for Critical Thinking.

Perkins, D. N. (1981). *The Mind's Best Work.* Cambridge, Mass.: Harvard University Press.

Plato. (1952). *The Dialogues of Plato.* Chicago: Encyclopedia Britannica.

"Poll Finds Americans Are Ignorant of Science." (October 25, 1988). *New York Times,* p. C10.

Polya, G. (1957). *How to Solve It.* New York: Anchor Books.

Poplin, M. (Spring 1984). "Summary Rationalizations, Apologies and Farewell: What We Don't Know About the Learning Disabled." *Learning Disability Quarterly* 7, 2: 133.

Proust, M. (1928). *Swan's Way.* New York: Modern Library.

Rose, C. (1987). *Accelerated Learning.* New York: Dell.

Rosenthal, R., and L. Jacobsen. (1968). *Pygmalion in the Classroom.* New York: Holt, Rinehart and Winston.

Rozin, P., S. Poritsky, and R. Sotsky. (March 26, 1971). "American Children with Reading Problems Can Easily Learn to Read English Represented by Chinese Characters." *Science* 171: 1264–1267.

Spolin, V. (1986). *Theater Games for the Classroom.* Evanston, Ill.: Northwestern University Press.

Stainback, S., W. Stainback, and M. Forest, eds. (1989). *Educating All Students in the Mainstream of Regular Education.* Baltimore, Md.: Paul H. Brookes.

Steiner, R. (1964). *The Kingdom of Childhood.* London: Rudolf Steiner Press.

Viadero, D. (March 13, 1991). "Music and Arts Courses Disappearing from Curriculum, Commission Warns." *Education Week,* p. 4.

Walters, J., and H. Gardner. (1986). "The Crystallizing Experience: Discovery of an Intellectual Gift." In *Conceptions of Giftedness,* edited by R. Sternberg and J. Davidson. New York: Cambridge University Press.

Weinreich-Haste, H. (1985). "The Varieties of Intelligence: An Interview with Howard Gardner." *New Ideas in Psychology* 3, 4: 47–65.

Weinstein, C. (1979). "The Physical Environment of the School: A Review of the Research." *Review of Educational Research* 49, 4: 585.

Wolf, D. P., P.G. LeMahieu, and J. Eresh. (May 1992). "Good Measure: Assessment as a Tool for Educational Reform." *Educational Leadership* 49, 8: 8–13.

APPENDIX A

A Basic Reading List on the Multiple Intelligences

Armstrong, Thomas. (1987). *In Their Own Way: Discovering and Encouraging Your Child's Personal Learning Style.* Los Angeles, Calif.: Jeremy P. Tarcher. A good introduction to multiple intelligences for parents and teachers.

Armstrong, Thomas. (1993). *7 Kinds of Smart: Discovering and Using Your Natural Intelligences.* New York: Plume/Penguin. The first book on multiple intelligences for the general public with self-help exercises and several checklists.

Campbell, Linda, Bruce Campbell, and Dee Dickinson. (1993). *Teaching and Learning Through Multiple Intelligences.* Tucson, Ariz.: Zephyr Press. Excellent source of teaching strategies in the five neglected intelligences (musical, spatial, bodily-kinesthetic, interpersonal, and intrapersonal).

Faggella, Kathy, and Janet Horowitz. (September 1990). "Different Child, Different Style." *Instructor* 100, 2: 49–54. A good short article on the instructional applications of MI theory.

Gardner, Howard. (1983). *Frames of Mind: The Theory of Multiple Intelligences.* New York: Basic Books. This is the bible of multiple intelligences. For more information on Gardner's research in MI Theory, write: Project Zero, Harvard University, Longfellow Hall, Appian Way, Cambridge, MA 02138.

Gardner, Howard. (1991). *To Open Minds.* New York: Basic Books. This book provides background information on the origins of multiple-intelligence theory.

Gardner, Howard. (1993). *Multiple Intelligences: The Theory in Practice.* New York: Basic Books. This book consists of a number of papers written by Gardner and his associates on MI theory updated to reflect his current thinking. Includes the best overall bibliography available on MI theory plus a list of consultants working in the field.

Gardner, Howard, and Thomas Hatch. (November/December 1988). "New Research on Intelligence." *Learning* 17, 4: 37-39. Good introductory article on MI theory for teachers just finding out about it. An excellent article to put up in the teacher's lounge.

Gardner, Howard, and Thomas Hatch. (November 1989). "Multiple Intelligences Go to School." *Educational Researcher* 18, 8: 4–10. Includes good research data on multiple intelligences in the schools.

Kline, Peter. (1988). *The Everyday Genius.* Arlington, Va.: Great Ocean. A book that is mainly about accelerated learning strategies but includes MI theory as an important component.

Kovalik, Susan. (1993). *ITI: The Model—Integrated Thematic Instruction.* Village of Oak Creek, Ariz.: Books for Educators. (Available from: Books for Educators, 17051 S.E. 277th St., Suite 18, Kent, WA 98032.) This book is primarily about integrated thematic instruction but includes a section on using MI theory in building thematic units.

Lazear, David. (1991). *Seven Ways of Knowing: Teaching for Multiple Intelligences.* Palatine, Ill.: Skylight. This is a very teacher-friendly introduction to the theory of multiple intelligences with many general activities for awakening and developing the intelligences. David Lazear also edits Intelligence Connections, a newsletter of ASCD's Multiple Intelligences Network. Write: David Lazear, New Dimensions of Learning, 729 W. Waveland, Suite G, Chicago, IL 60613. Or call (312) 525-6650.

Lazear, David. (1991). *Seven Ways of Teaching: The Artistry of Teaching with Multiple Intelligences.* Palatine, Ill.: Skylight. A book containing seven detailed lesson plans; each chapter focuses on teaching a school subject through one of the seven intelligences (e.g., teaching geometry through bodily-kinesthetic intelligence).

Lazear, David. (1993). *Seven Pathways of Learning: Teaching Students and Parents about Multiple Intelligences.* Tucson, Ariz.: Zephyr Press. Includes reproducible activities and lesson extensions for teaching about multiple intelligences.

Lazear, David. (1994). *Multiple Intelligence Approaches to Assessment: Solving the Assessment Conundrum.* Tucson, Ariz.: Zephyr Press. Instruction on creating student intelligence profiles, processfolios, reflective journals and logs, checklists, and multiperceptual formal tests.

Teele, Sue. (1991). *Teaching and Assessment Strategies Appropriate for the Multiple Intelligences.* Riverside, Calif.: University of California Extension. (Available from: University of California Extension, H101 Bannockburn, University of California, Riverside, CA 92521-0112.) Sue Teele directs a Multiple Intelligences Certificate Program at U.C. Riverside and has authored an assessment device for MI theory called the TIMI (Teele Inventory of Multiple Intelligences). Write to her at: UCR Extension Center, 1200 University Ave., Riverside, CA 92507-4596.

Thornburg, David. (1989). *The Role of Technology in Teaching to the Whole Child: Multiple Intelligences in the Classroom.* Los Altos, Calif.: Starsong Publications. Thornburg applies here his substantial background in computer technology (he helped develop the Muppet Learning Keys and the Koala Pad) to MI theory.

Wass, Lane Longino. (1991). *Imagine That: Getting Smarter Through Imagery Practice.* Rolling Hills Estate, Calif.: Jalmar Press. MI theory applied to guided imagery.

Winn, Marie. (April 29, 1990). "New Views of Human Intelligence." *New York Times Magazine,* pp. 16+. A good popular article to send to school board members.

Related Books on MI Teaching

Linguistic Intelligence

Ashton-Warner, Sylvia. (1986). *Teacher*. New York: Simon & Schuster.

Bissex, Glenda. (1980). *Gnys at Work: A Child Learns to Write and Read*. Cambridge, Mass.: Harvard University Press.

Graves, Donald, and Virginia Stuart. (1987). *Write from the Start: Tapping Your Child's Natural Writing Ability*. New York: NAL.

Rico, Gabrielle Lusser. (1983). *Writing the Natural Way*. Los Angeles: Jeremy P. Tarcher.

Trelease, Jim. (1982). *The Read-Aloud Handbook*. Harmondsworth, England: Penguin.

Logical-Mathematical Intelligence

Allison, Linda. (1976). *Blood and Guts: A Working Guide to Your Own Insides*. Boston: Little, Brown & Co. Grades 5–12. See also other books in Brown Paper School Book series.

Burns, Marilyn. (1975). *The I Hate Mathematics! Book*. Boston: Little, Brown & Co.

Jacobs, Harold. (1982). *Mathematics: A Human Endeavor*. San Francisco: W. H. Freeman. Grades 9–12.

Lorton, Mary Baratta. (1976). *Mathematics Their Way*. Menlo Park, Calif.: Addison-Wesley.

Stein, Sara. (1980). *The Science Book*. New York: Workman. Grades 4–7.

Spatial Intelligence

DeMille, Richard. (1981). *Put Your Mother on the Ceiling: Children's Imagination Games*. Santa Barbara, Calif.: Santa Barbara Press.

Edwards, Betty. (1979). *Drawing on the Right Side of the Brain*. Los Angeles: Jeremy P. Tarcher.

McKim, Robert H. (1980). *Experiences in Visual Thinking*. Monterey, Calif.: Brooks-Cole. High school level.

Samples, Robert. (1976). *The Metaphoric Mind*. Reading, Mass.: Addison-Wesley.

Warner, Sally. (1989). *Encouraging the Artist in Your Child*. New York: St. Martin's Press.

Bodily-Kinesthetic Intelligence

Benzwie, Teresa. (1988). *A Moving Experience: Dance for Lovers of Children and the Child Within*. Tucson, Ariz.: Zephyr Press.

Cobb, Vicki. (1972). *Science Experiments You Can Eat.* Philadelphia: Lippincott.
Gilbert, Anne G. (1977). *Teaching the 3 R's Through Movement Experiences.* New York: Macmillan.
Schneider, Tom. (1976). *Everybody's a Winner: A Kids' Guide to New Sports and Fitness.* Boston: Little, Brown & Co.
Spolin, Viola. (1986). *Theater Games for the Classroom.* Evanston, Ill.: Northwestern University Press.

Musical Intelligence

Bonny, Helen, and Louis Savary. (1990). *Music and Your Mind.* Barrytown, N.Y.: Station Hill Press.
Brewer, Chris Boyd, and Don G. Campbell. (1991). *Rhythms of Learning.* Tucson, Ariz.: Zephyr Press.
Halpern, Steven, and Savary Louis. (1985). *Sound Health: Music and Sounds That Make Us Whole.* San Francisco: Harper and Row.
Judy, Stephanie. (1990). *Making Music for the Joy of It.* Los Angeles: Jeremy P. Tarcher.
Merritt, Stephanie. (1990). *Mind, Music, and Imagery: 40 Exercises Using Music to Stimulate Creativity and Self-Awareness.* New York: NAL/Plume.
Wallace, Rosella R. (1992). *Rappin' and Rhymin': Raps, Songs, Cheers, and SmartRope Jingles for Active Learning.* Tucson, Ariz.: Zephyr Press.

Interpersonal Intelligence

Johnson, David W., Roger T. Johnson, and Edythe Johnson Holubec. (1986). *Circles of Learning: Cooperation in the Classroom.* Alexandria, VA.: ASCD.
Orlick, Terry. (1978). *The Cooperative Sports and Games Book.* New York: Pantheon.
Sobel, Jeffrey. (1983). *Everybody Wins: 393 Non-Competitive Games for Young Children.* New York: Walker and Co.
Weinstein, Matt, and Joel Goodman. (1980). *Playfair: Everybody's Guide to Noncompetitive Play.* San Luis Obispo, Calif.: Impact.
Wade, Rahima Carol. (1991). *Joining Hands: From Personal to Planetary Friendship in the Primary Classroom.* Tucson, Ariz.: Zephyr Press.

Intrapersonal Intelligence

Armstrong, Thomas. (1985). *The Radiant Child.* Wheaton, Ill.: Quest.
Briggs, Dorothy Corkille. (1970). *Your Child's Self-Esteem.* Garden City, N.Y.: Doubleday.
Canfield, Jack, and Wells, Harold C. (1976). *100 Ways to Enhance Self-Esteem in the Classroom.* Englewood Cliffs, N.J.: Prentice-Hall.
Gibbons, Maurice. (1991). *How to Become an Expert: Discover, Research, and Build a Project in Your Chosen Field.* Tucson, Ariz.: Zephyr Press.
Oaklander, Violet. (1978). *Windows to Our Children.* Moab, Utah: Real People Press.

APPENDIX C

Examples of MI Lessons and Programs

The following examples of lessons and programs based upon MI theory are designed for a variety of different grade levels. Note that in some cases, MI theory is used to provide the basis for the development of a program (e.g., a primary-level reading list); in other cases, MI theory is limited to the development of ideas that can be incorporated into existing curricular frameworks. In some cases, the educational focus is on the development of skills (e.g., learning how to multiply by 7); in other cases, the emphasis is more on concepts (e.g., understanding Boyle's law). In every lesson, however, activities spanning all seven intelligences have been used to achieve the given instructional objective.

Example One

Level: Preschool
Subject: Shapes
Objective: To teach students to recognize circles.

Students will experience different types of circles in the following ways (the emphasized intelligence appears in brackets):

- Make a group circle by joining hands. [Interpersonal, Bodily-Kinesthetic]
- Make circles by using their bodies. [Intrapersonal, Bodily-Kinesthetic]
- Look for circles around the classroom. [Spatial]
- Make circles in art projects. [Spatial, Bodily-Kinesthetic]
- Sing "The Circle Game" and other circle songs (including "rounds," which are themselves musically circular). [Musical]
- Make up stories about circles. [Linguistic]
- Compare sizes of circles (from small to large). [Spatial, Logical-Mathematical]

Example Two

Level: Kindergarten–1st grade
Subject: Reading
Objective: To help develop a "book positive" attitude in students

Materials: Books that combine linguistic intelligence with one or more other intelligences

A classroom library will be stocked with books of the following types (the emphasized intelligence appears in brackets):

- Books with read-along cassettes [Linguistic]
- Three-dimensional pop-up books [Spatial]
- Wordless books (pictorial stories) [Spatial]
- Touch 'n' feel books [Bodily-Kinesthetic]
- Books with sing-along cassettes [Musical]
- Books with computerized keyboards and song lyrics [Musical]
- Science fun books [Logical-Mathematical]
- Counting books [Logical-Mathematical]
- "This-is-me" type of books [Intrapersonal]
- Books on emotional themes, such as loss or anger [Intrapersonal]
- Interactive books [Interpersonal]

Example Three

Level: 2nd–3rd grade
Subject: Math
Objectives: To help students master the multiplication table facts for the 7's; also, to reinforce the concept of what it means to "multiply."

The class will do one of these activities each day during math class (the emphasized intelligence appears in brackets):

- Count to 70, standing up and clapping on every seventh number. [Bodily-Kinesthetic]

- Sing the Multiplication Rock song for the 7's. [Musical]

- Chant the numbers 1 to 70, placing special emphasis on every seventh number. [Musical]

- Complete a "hundreds chart," coloring in every seventh number. [Spatial]

- Form circles of ten students, each student wearing a number from 0 to 9. Starting with the 0, participants count off as they go around the circle (the second time around the circle, the 0 becomes a 10, the 1 an 11, and so on; the third time around, the 0 becomes a 20, the 1 a 21, and so on). As they count, participants pass a ball of yarn around the circle, unrolling it as they do so. The first person grasps the end of the yarn, and every seventh person after that also grasps a section before passing the ball of yarn on. On reaching the count of 70, students will see that the yarn creates a geometric design. [Spatial, Bodily-Kinesthetic, Interpersonal]

- Create their own geometric designs for the 7's on a geoboard or in a drawing using the strategy described above (e.g., use a circle numberd 0 to 9 and then connect with string or a line every seventh number up to 70). [Spatial]

• Listen to a story about "The As Much Brothers" (who can touch things and see them multiply; for instance, when Seven Times As Much touches 3 golden hens, 21 golden hens appear). [Linguistic]

• Create "before" and "after" drawings based on The As Much Brothers story (for instance, Seven Times As Much just before touching the 3 golden hens and just after touching them). [Spatial]

Example Four

Level: Upper Elementary
Subject: History
Objective: To assist students in understanding the conditions that led to the development of Rhode Island in early American history

Students will engage in one or more of the following activities each day during history period (the intelligences emphasized appear in brackets):

• Read textbook passages that give reasons for the settling of Rhode Island and discuss their readings. [Linguistic]

• Create a time line of the events surrounding the development of Rhode Island. [Logical-Mathematical, Spatial]

• Study maps of the United States during the colonial era showing the progressive development of Rhode Island. [Spatial]

• Compare the settling of Rhode Island with the growth of an amoeba. [Spatial]

• Act out the events surrounding the settling of Rhode Island. [Bodily-Kinesthetic, Interpersonal]

• Create a song that describes the circumstances leading to the settling of Rhode Island. [Musical]

• Divide into groups representing different colonies; groups then relate to the development of another group of students as Rhode Island. [Interpersonal, Bodily-Kinesthetic]

• Relate the settling of Rhode Island to their own need or desire to break away from authority at times (e.g.. conflicts with parents/teachers). [Intrapersonal]

Example Five

Level: Junior High School
Subject: Algebra
Objective: To explain the function of x in an equation

• Students are provided with a verbal description of x ("x is an unknown"). [Linguistic]

• Students are given an equation (e.g., $2x + 1 = 5$) and shown how to solve for x. [Logical-Mathematical]

• Students are told that x is like a masked outlaw that needs to be unmasked; students draw their own version of x. [Spatial]

• Students act out an algebraic equation, where a student wearing a mask plays x, and other students represent numbers or functions; a designated student then "solves" the equation by removing students on both sides of the equation in a series of steps. For instance, in the equation $2x + 1 = 5$, one student is removed from the left side, and one from the right, then half the students are removed from the right, and half from the left, revealing x as 4. [Interpersonal; Bodily-Kinesthetic]

• Students perform algebraic equations using manipulatives (numbers and functions on a scale; sides must be kept in balance in order to solve). [Bodily-Kinesthetic]

• Students rhythmically repeat the following lyrics several times:

x is a mystery
you've gotta find a way
to get him all alone
so he's gotta say his name

Students can accompany their chanting with any available percussion instruments. [Musical]

• Students are asked, "What are the mysteries—or x's—in your own life?" Discuss how students "solve for x" in dealing with personal issues. [Intrapersonal]

Example Six

Level: High School
Subject: Chemistry
Objective: To teach the concept of Boyle's Law

• Students are provided with a verbal definition of Boyle's Law: "For a fixed mass and temperature of gas, the pressure is inversely proportional to the volume." They discuss the definition. [Linguistic]

• Students are given a formula that describes Boyle's Law: $P \times V = K$. They solve specific problems connected to it. [Logical-Mathematical]

• Students are given a metaphor or visual image for Boyle's law: "Imagine that you have a boil on your hand that you start to squeeze. As you squeeze it, the pressure builds. The more you squeeze, the higher the pressure, until the boil finally bursts and puss spurts out all over your hand!" [Spatial]

• Students do the following experiment: They breathe air into their mouths so that their cheeks puff up slightly. Then they put all the air into one side of their mouth (less volume) and indicate whether pressure goes up or down (it goes up); then they're asked to release the air into both sides of their mouth (more volume) and asked to indicate whether pressure has gone up or down (it goes down). [Bodily-Kinesthetic]

- Students rhythmically repeat the following musical mnemonic:

When the volume goes down
The pressure goes up
The blood starts to boil
And a scream erupts
'I need more space
Or I'm going to frown'
The volume goes up
And the pressure goes down

[Musical]

- Students become "molecules" of air in a "container" (a clearly defined corner of the classroom). They move at a constant rate (temperature) and cannot leave the container (constant mass). Gradually the size of the container is reduced as two volunteers holding a piece of yarn representing one side of the container start moving it in on the "people molecules." The smaller the space, the more pressure (i.e., bumping into each other) is observed; the greater the space, the less pressure. [Interpersonal, Bodily-Kinesthetic]

- Students do lab experiments that measure air pressure in sealed containers and chart pressure against volume. [Logical-Mathematical, Bodily-Kinesthetic]

- Students are asked about times in their lives when they were "under pressure": "Did you feel like you had a lot of space?" (Typical answer: lots of pressure/not much space.) Then students are asked about times when they felt little pressure (little pressure/ lots of space). Students' experiences are related to Boyle's Law. [Intrapersonal]

Index

179

ASCD Resources on
Multiple Intelligences

ASCD Network

Teaching for Multiple Intelligences Network. For information, contact David G. Lazear, facilitator, 729 West Waveland, Suite G, Chicago, IL 60613. Telephone: (312) 525-6650.

Educational Leadership

Theme issue on untracking for equity. In addition to articles on tracking, includes features on ability grouping, nongraded schools, gifted children and cooperative learning, learning modalities and multiple intelligences, self-directed learners, and the use of film in language arts. October 1992 (vol. 50, no. 2), stock no. 611-92148. $5.00.

Theme issue on restructuring. In an article called ''A School for All Intelligences,'' Tina Blythe and Howard Gardner describe pilot projects that use MI theory in the classroom; they encourage educators to apply MI theory and practices as they bring about school reform and restructuring. April 1990 (vol. 47, no. 7), stock no. 611-90003. $5.00.

Audiocassette

The Proper Assessment of Multiple Intelligences. Howard Gardner explains why the traditional assessment techniques used in schools are inadequate for assessing multiple intelligences. He considers how Albert Einstein, Picasso, and Virginia Woolf might be measured by the traditional assessment techniques used in schools today. ASCD stock no. 612-91101. $9.95.

Please remember that this is a library book,
and that it belongs only temporarily to each
person who uses it. Be considerate. Do
not write in this, or any, library book.